Saltman's book takes us into new excess and repression that focus on the possibilities of teaching and learning – that is, the erasure of thinking. This is a nightmare world of apps, performance-enhancing drugs and big business. Drawing on a wide range of theoretical resources and up-to-the-minute data, this book is both terrifying and analytically stunning.

Stephen J. Ball, Institute of Education, University of London

In *Scripted Bodies*, Ken Saltman offers an engaging analysis of how pedagogical strategies easily become repressive. Saltman focuses on how 'new' pedagogies manipulate students' corporeal selves, an essential counterpoint to the ubiquitous psychological and behavioral orientations to cognitive and social-emotional aspects of learning and development. This book breaks down the mind-body distinction that permeates pedagogy, and situates pedagogy within a socio-political context defined by corporations and technologies. Saltman ends on a hopeful note of resistance to recapture genuine democratic conditions for schooling and beyond.

Sandra Mathison, Faculty of Education, University of British Columbia

This is possibly Saltman's masterwork. It's a heart-pounding and eye-opening account of the discipline-and-punish pedagogy that our children endure in nearly all walks of life. This is no theoretical tale, but a keenly observed documentation of the horrifying but real ways schools control children's bodies in order to control their minds.

Marc Bousquet, author of *How the University Works*, and professor of Film and Media, Emory University

SCRIPTED BODIES

From drugging kids into attention and reviving behaviorism to biometric measurements of teaching and learning, *Scripted Bodies* exposes a brave new world of education in the age of repression. *Scripted Bodies* examines how corporeal control has expanded in education, how it impacts the mind and thinking, and the ways that new technologies are integral to the expansion of control.

Scripted Bodies contends that this rise in repression must be understood in relation to the broader economic, political, and cultural forces that have produced an increasingly authoritarian society. This book details how these new forms of corporeal control shut down the possibility of public schools developing as places where thinking becomes the organizing principle needed to contribute to a more equal, just, and democratic society.

Kenneth J. Saltman is a professor in the Department of Educational Leadership at the University of Massachusetts, Dartmouth, where he teaches courses in the Educational Leadership and Policy Studies PhD program.

Critical Interventions

SCRIPTED BODIES

Corporate Power, Smart Technologies, and the Undoing of Public Education

Kenneth J. Saltman

 Routledge
Taylor & Francis Group

NEW YORK AND LONDON

First published 2017
by Routledge
711 Third Avenue, New York, NY 10017

and by Routledge
2 Park Square, Milton Park, Abingdon, Oxon, OX14 4RN

Routledge is an imprint of the Taylor & Francis Group, an informa business

© 2017 Taylor & Francis

Library of Congress Cataloging in Publication Data
    Names: Saltman, Kenneth J., 1969- author.
    Title: Scripted bodies : corporate power, smart technology, and the undoing of public education / Kenneth J. Saltman.
    Description: New York, NY : Routledge, 2016. | Series: Critical interventions
    Identifiers: LCCN 2016004038| ISBN 9781138675261 (hardback) | ISBN 9781138675278 (pbk.) | ISBN 9781315560793 (ebook)
    Subjects: LCSH: Educational sociology. | School management and organization--Social aspects. | Educational technology-- Social aspects. | Corporatization. | Privatization in education. | Business and education.
    Classification: LCC LC191 .S1655 2016 | DDC 306.430973--dc23
    LC record available at https://lccn.loc.gov/2016004038

ISBN: 978-1-138-67526-1 (hbk)
ISBN: 978-1-138-67527-8 (pbk)
ISBN: 978-1-315-56079-3 (ebk)

Typeset in Bembo
by Sunrise Setting Ltd, Brixham, UK

Printed and bound in the United States of America by Publishers Graphics, LLC on sustainably sourced paper.

CONTENTS

ACKNOWLEDGMENTS

A few friends in particular played an outsized role in helping me to write this book. I am fortunate to have a far flung community of critical intellectuals. Among them my great friend Robin Truth Goodman spent an inordinate amount of time discussing ideas, suggesting reading, and editing all of the chapters. I cannot thank her enough. I had the benefit of discussing with Henry Giroux key ideas at both an early and late stage in the project. Henry is a terrific friend and an inspiration aside from being one of the most important cultural critics and educational thinkers. Alex Means discussed with me most of the chapters in their early form and had a big and valuable influence on the book. My colleague and friend Joao Paraskeva gave me the benefit of discussing ideas and made possible the work conditions that allowed me to do the project. I also want to especially thank the students in the Educational Leadership and Policy doctoral program at UMass Dartmouth with whom I discussed and presented much of what became this book. Their exchange and thoughtful insights contributed greatly to this project.

I am really pleased to have worked again with editor Dean Birkenkamp whose thoughtful input always benefits a project. I would also like to thank Routledge editorial assistant Amanda Yee.

A number of other friends, family members, and colleagues contributed in a variety of ways. Thanks to: Kathy Szybist, Simone Saltman, Sheila Macrine, Donaldo Macedo, Ricardo Rosa, Jeff Isaacs, Noah Gelfand, Kevin Bunka, Mark Garrison, David Hursh, Rob Isaacs, Michelle Decker, Ebony

Rose, Josh Shepperd, Mark Wolfmeyer, Joel Spring, Pauline Lipman, Enora Brown, Kate Way, Jeffrey Di Leo, and Al Lingis.

Artist Martin Senn generously provided the cover image of his sculpture *In the Penal Colony* that depicts the story by Franz Kafka.

Chapter 2: "The Austerity School: Grit, Character, and the Privatization of Public Education" appeared in *symplokē* 22(1–2).

An earlier version of Chapter 5: "Learning to Be a Psychopath: The Pedagogy of the Corporation" appeared in Masood Ashraf Raja, Hillary Stringer, and Zach Vandezande (editors) *Critical Pedagogy and Global Literature: Worldly Teaching*, New York: Palgrave Macmillan, in my series "New Frontiers in Education, Culture, and Politics" reproduced with permission of Palgrave Macmillan.

I wish to reassure readers that all of the URLs are current as of February 15, 2016.

INTRODUCTION

Scripted Bodies: Corporate Power, Smart Technologies, and the Undoing of Public Education

Repressive Education Turns to the Body

The US media frequently showcases China's test-preparation madness. In 2014, images circulated of cramming Chinese youth hooked up to intravenous drip bags hung on chrome poles. Students in cram factories, private test-prep institutions preparing for the national college entrance exam, received hydration and nutrients from these IV drips in order to avoid wasting time eating and drinking. The images did not make clear how students, who were too focused on cramming to eat or drink, would be taking care of the excretive results. The outcomes of the exams determine placement at elite universities and then coveted jobs, or regional colleges and less auspicious employment, or a life of sweeping the streets. In 2015, images appeared of Chinese military style drones being flown by the government over students taking these high stakes tests to detect mobile transmissions from high technology cheating devices, such as purloined cell phones, eyeglasses modified with computer chips, and secreted screens. These widely circulated images of the medical manipulation and military surveillance of masses of young bodies evoke dystopian stories from film and television and, of course, from George Orwell's novel *Nineteen Eighty-Four*. *We*, these stories in the US mass media suggest, would never do this to *our* children.

Yet, for the past three decades, US schools have embraced ever more repressive controls over their physical space that now include the arrests of young children, prison technologies, metal detectors, arming teachers, drugging students, biometric tracking systems, "close-captioned" TV surveillance systems, both in and out of school, Zero Tolerance, police in schools, schools run as military academies, and military personnel recruited to teach and lead. These spaces of control are accompanied by repressive pedagogies that not only standardize the curriculum, time, and space of school but also control the bodies of youth and teachers. Repressive pedagogies include the eradication of recess, strict bodily behavior codes in the classroom and in the hall, heavy testing and teaching to the test, behaviorist cues in teaching, and the implementation of scripted lessons. The rise of repression in schooling has social and individual costs that include not only the expansion of educationally dubious pedagogical approaches but also the promotion of hierarchical, authoritarian, and anti-democratic dispositions and social relationships. Repressive pedagogy positions learning as submission to authority and knowledge as the domain and product of the powerful. These practices and policies are implicated in producing particular kinds of selves and fostering a particular kind of society.

This book details and criticizes a number of startling and spectacular new repressive educational technologies, including drugging children to compete in examinations, applying behaviorist techniques of bodily control (grit) for the same purpose, measuring teacher performance by wiring children to biometric measurement devices, and replacing teachers and professors with hardware and software. While not all of these "smart technologies" are universally implemented, each chapter explains how the assumptions, values, and ideologies behind these techniques of control are in fact dominant, widespread, and the norm.

For example, assumptions of knowledge as a deliverable commodity, teachers as delivery agents, and students as knowledge consumers are codified in the approach to knowledge, the self, and society in all of the major recent educational policies such as the revised teacher education accreditation body CAEP (Council for the Accreditation of Educator Preparation) formerly NCATE (National Council for Accreditation of Teacher Education), the Pearson-run student teaching assessment platform edTPA, and the Common Core State Standards. Specifically these policies share an approach to learning and knowledge characterized by an active denial of how knowledge relates to the experience and subjectivity of students and teachers. These policies are also united in their refusal of how learning and knowledge relate to the world and the capacity of subjects to use knowledge to shape it. That is, dominant educational policies presume a conception of agency in which the social power of the individual derives from the acquisition and exchange of socially consecrated knowledge. Agency in this view does not stem from the use of knowledge to interpret, judge, act on, and shape the social world while reflecting on what one does. Instead, agency appears as consumption and display of knowledge for academic promotion and later material consumption. This is not a nostalgic lament for the loss of thinking from public schooling. Much of what has historically gone on in public schools has suffered from hostility to thinking as I define it here. However, the new forms of control that this book details shut down the possibility for public schools to develop as places where thinking (self and social reflectiveness, analysis, and theorization that can form the basis for agency) becomes the organizing principle of the school and can contribute to a more equal, just, and democratic society. Moreover, each of the chapters in this book examines how corporeal control has expanded in education, how it impacts the mind and thinking, and the ways that different technologies are integral to these new expressions of control. The new forms of control over bodies that this book details are about controlling bodies for the purpose of controlling minds.

Situating the Rise of Repressive Education: The Economic

The expansion of corporeal control in public education is inseparable from the broader repressive social turn found in militarized policing, the state of permanent war, mass incarceration of prisoners and immigrants, dispossession of communities through the destruction of public schools and housing, and so on. Rising repression in public education cannot be understood apart from the powerful economic forces driving it. William I. Robinson makes a compelling case that the inherent crises of capitalist accumulation in a continually globalizing economy require management for the transnational capitalist class to maintain its global hegemony.[1] The management of these crises, including the most recent one of 2008, requires the use of force—what Stuart Hall referred to in the context of the United Kingdom of the 1970s as "policing the crisis." As well, the capitalist crisis of overaccumulation results in the conditions whereby the private sector pillages the public sector as it seeks out new markets. The crisis of overaccumulation has also driven disaster politics in which profit accumulation strategies have been sought through destruction (Iraq, Katrina, educational defunding) and the making of an increasingly disposable workforce and population.[2] The same forces have been at work in the last 30 years of the neoliberal divestment from the social state and investment in the repressive arm of the state. Public education is one such place that has been positioned as ripe for pillage with multiple forms of privatizations—charters, vouchers, scholarship tax credits, commercialism, and contracting. For profit forms of schooling not only disproportionately target working class and poor students but they also tend towards pedagogies of repression and standardized approaches to teaching and learning.

Nancy Fraser, David Harvey, and others have pointed to a rise in repression caused by the crisis of social and cultural reproduction.[3] That is, changes in capitalist production have changed the kinds of social relationships necessary to reproduce capital. Managed through Keynesian assumptions, the Fordist industrial economy involved a compact between labor and capital, a role for the welfare state, and the need for learned self-regulation in forms that were time and labor intensive. For example, the school produced knowledge and skills for the labor force but wrapped them in ideologies conducive for students to take their prescribed places in the workforce. Workers learned discipline, docility, and obedience to authority while future managers learned to question and engage in dialogue. Learned self-control played a prominent role in Fordist forms of self- and social control. The shift to the post-Fordist economy involved not only the departure of industrial production to cheap manufacturing zones, the shift to the service and financial economy, the flexible insecure labor force, and de-unionization. It also revised social and cultural reproduction in order to create social relations for capital accumulation.

Reproduction decreasingly involved the time and labor intensive strategies of self-control that were characteristic of Fordism, such as the talking cure of psychoanalysis, the rehabilitative aims of the prison, and the long slow process of making docile subjects in the school through socialization. With post-Fordism came direct management of the body, yet in different class-based forms. Professional class workers need to be entrepreneurial self-managing subjects of capacity who can administer forms of bodily self-control as they have only themselves to rely upon. Amid increasingly precarious economic conditions in the globalizing economy—declining incomes, lack of a safety net, precarity, the disinvestment in the social state, and the investment in the punishing state—working class workers have become increasingly subject to repressive control that targets the body itself. The psychoanalytic couch is eclipsed by the anti-depressant and anti-anxiety pill. The prison is transformed from the scene of learned rehabilitation to a place where the body is locked away in isolation. The school comes to look increasingly like the prison and the military: lock up, cops, CCTV, and pills replace counselors and bureaucratically overwhelmed teachers as the bodies of working class youth of color become targets for direct control.

Professional class youth must learn to modify, modulate, and manage control over their own bodies and moods for performance and capacity, especially on standardized tests and to display mastery of standardized knowledge. Learned self-regulation takes an increasingly corporeal form as anxiety medication is joined by amphetamine attention control drugs for the self-managed neoliberal entrepreneurial subject in the new conditions of economic and social precarity. For working class youth, the same attention drugs are prescribed to keep kids quiet and still and to prevent them from distracting other controlled bodies in test-preparation mode. The racialized class-based pattern that plays out in the registers of testing, curriculum, and pharmacology takes a similar form in the domain of technological surveillance. Predominantly White professional class youth learn that to compete socially, educationally, and ultimately economically, they must learn to manage control over the televisual image of their bodies and personas for others to watch on social media. Working class non-White and White youth are subject to the criminological gaze of technological surveillance that interpellates them as bad subjects from the get-go. And while learned self-control of the Fordist variety has not disappeared, it is wrapped up with numerical metrics, the standardization of knowledge, and the growing use of technology.

All of this control comes at a social cost. Social interaction, including teaching and learning, decreasingly takes the form of dialogue, questioning, investigation, debate, and dissent, the crucial dispositions for democratic, thoughtful, and self-reflective society. Instead, repression towards the end of obedience to authority becomes paramount. Of course, all of this repression in its pharmacological, technological, curricular, and pedagogical forms is big, big business. For example, the industry in attention control amphetamine attention deficit hyperactivity disorder (ADHD) drugs that exploded with the launch of high stakes standardized testing is now the most lucrative segment of pharmaceuticals—a US$13 billion a year business expected to reach US$17.5 billion by 2020.[4] Educational technology products that aim to replace teachers with tablets and computer programs are expected to double to US$13.7 billion by 2017, propelled by the Common Core State Standards which themselves are a massive part of a massive multi-billion dollar educational test and textbook industry benefitting a few massive corporations such as Pearson NCS, Houghton–Mifflin, Educational Testing Service, and Kaplan.[5] As the chapters of this book detail, attention capture drugs, corporate curricular standardization products, and repression and surveillance technologies in schools each are multi-billion dollar industries, and as the chapters on grit and biometrics and learning analytics detail, new control products, industries, and approaches are being steadily developed. For example, as this book goes to press, the 2015 federal Every Student Succeeds Act passed. This law is the latest release of the Elementary and Secondary Education Act that updates No Child Left Behind. It has, on the one hand, shifted the federal power over test-based accountability to the states and local authorities. While this would appear to decrease the heavy-handed federal role in high stakes standardized testing, it also maintains requirements for test-based forms of accountability at the state level. It also federally supports the launch of "pay for success" or "social impact bond" schemes and "social emotional learning" schemes like projects to promote "grit." "Pay for success" schemes allow investment banks such as Goldman Sachs to "invest" in educational services and collect additional public money as profits if these projects meet accountability metrics. Venture philanthropies, especially the Rockefeller Foundation, are championing these schemes that appeal to politicians because they can claim they are funding social services without raising taxes. Investors love them because they can capture public money by gaming the metrics and make a fortune from getting a bonus payment from the public entity. This allows for stealth privatization and public resource skimming while relying on heavy amounts of surveillance and numerically quantifiable accountability schemes to justify the skimming. So while the federal government partly withdraws from directly punishing the poor through testing under ESSA, it requires states to continue testing, and it funds and promotes new forms of privatization, surveillance, and corporeal control over students and teachers. It also privatizes teacher and leadership preparation by promoting alternative certification that undermines the role of universities and expands private practitioner-oriented forms of preparation linked to charters and other private school operators. Hence, the restoration of local control in the forms it takes in the ESSA offers new insidious forms of control. Together, these reforms set the stage for forms of K12 education that run counter to precisely the kinds of intellectual tools that teachers and students need to theorize their experiences and social contexts in order to be able to control, collectively act on, and transform the context they find themselves in. However, new state and local control over curriculum, pedagogy, and assessment do offer an opening for teachers, administrators, parents, and citizens to put in place critical pedagogical projects that can redefine and reclaim teaching and learning in ways that link knowledge to power and politics, learning to ethical action, and that situate learning in terms of broader social struggles and lived realities.

Two processes that are not reducible to each other are at play in the new constellation of control. Capitalist globalization results in a series of economic crises, worsening work opportunities and security. Transnational capitalists police the crisis, controlling and managing middle class, working class, and poor people. Such policing of the crisis involves producing knowledge in forms conducive to the interests and worldviews of economic and political elites. For example, "good" schooling is about individual opportunity and knowledge accumulation (that is, acquiring tidbits of useable knowledge as though knowledge were a series of ready-made objects for consumption). Ever greater control over the curriculum, teaching, time, and space come at the expense of socially transformative views of school that emphasize knowledge and learning as the basis for collective forms of agency and self-governance, ethical life, and the creation of a sustainable future free of domination. Policing the crisis also involves knowledge-making activities outside of schools.

Advertising driven mass media in particular plays a central role in forging the boundaries of debate that are ideologically acceptable to elites. Within these bounded debates in corporate mass media, openly authoritarian, White supremacist, and even fascist political views are increasingly presented as legitimate points of view in corporate mass media while serious and scholarly questions that breach the ideological boundaries are kept out of popular discourse. For example, some off-limit questions include the social and ecological costs of the continued use of fossil fuels, the inevitable ecological and human destruction of an economic system organized around unlimited capital accumulation, the material destruction resulting from a cultural system organized around the ideology of consumerism, the ways that ideologies of White supremacy structure institutions and domestic and foreign policy, and the assumed beneficence of an imperial US military that keeps corporate profits safe while furthering the precarity of human beings. As serious discussion of the social, systemic, and structural causes of human and environmental problems cannot be taken up in corporate educational and media discourse, emotionally potent simplifications, such as the scapegoating of groups of people, return to public and political discourse with a vengeance. Within such impoverished public and political discourse, corporeal control takes on inflated importance as the last recourse for Americans to respond to an inexplicable world of danger—building bigger walls, dropping more bombs, having more guns, making schools resemble prisons and model-ing social progress on the data analytics of spy agencies and the technol-ogies of war and policing.

The second crucial process at play in the new culture of control involves the expanding commodification of youth as pillaging the public sector creates new accumulation possibilities. My prior books have detailed this in its various forms. This book highlights several new forms of commodi-fication of youth, including pharmacology, grit, biometrics, tablet technol-ogy, and online analytic learning platforms. These technologies are united by the shared project of corporeal control of students and teachers, the aim of replacing dialogue and reflection with the measurement of bodies, and a hostility to the development of critical consciousness that would create the conditions for learning to be the basis for understanding and acting on the social world with others.

Slavoj Žižek, informed by a group of Italian autonomists such as Car-los Vercellone, Christian Marazzi, and Maurizio Lazzarato among others, offers an economic explanation of rising repression that derives from the prominence of information technology, the free exchange of knowledge and information, and the difficulty that nation-states have in enforcing ownership rights through rent.[6] This theoretical trend attempts to come to terms with the transformations to labor, subjectivity, and capital accumu-lation in post-Fordism. In this view, influenced by Marx's "Fragment on Machines" from his *Grundrisse*, the knowledge economy presents a prob-lem to traditional forms of profit accumulation in the form of extracting value from exploited labor. In the economy of sharing and free exchange, state repression steps in on behalf of capital to assure profits by enforcing intellectual property rights. The structural realities of capitalism produce recurrent economic crises, steadily declining real wages, record levels of income and wealth inequality. Yet, rising repression cannot be understood as a mere effect or response to allegedly natural and inevitable economic realities and new technologies. In the last 40 years, ruling class people fought and won politically and culturally to enact policies and revise laws to transform common sense to make possible unprecedented upward redistributions of wealth and repressive apparatuses justified in the inter-ests of universal benefit. As the most successful investor and second rich-est American Warren Buffett succinctly put it in 2011, "Actually, there's been class warfare going on for the last 20 years, and my class has won."[7] Economic and political elites fought and won tax cuts for the rich, the deregulation of banks and financial markets, investment in prisons rather than schools, the disinvestment in public housing, public schools, public healthcare, public mental health facilities, the launching of unjustifiable trillion dollar wars, the transfer onto students of a trillion dollar higher education debt burden, and the deregulation of campaign finance. These triumphs of financial and political elites that came at the cost of the poor, working class, and lower professional class were hardly inevitable nor were they a mere effect of the structural tendencies of the economy. It is crucial to remember that elites and their traditional intellectuals painstakingly achieved these reactionary gains through educational work. However, the gains are fragile. They can only be maintained by the ongoing use of both force and ideology and they can be reversed.

Situating the Rise of Repression Education: The Political

In the United States the growing repression in education must be linked to the dramatic erosion of popular political sovereignty and the ascendancy of market sovereignty. The vast majority of citizens take on only a spectator role in the workings of their government. The US Supreme Court's 2010 decision in "Citizens United v. FEC (Federal Election Commission)" only deepened a system of money driven elections determined by mass media advertising. Electoral politics has come to be so dominated by purchased advertising and strategy that winning the presidency costs more than a billion dollars. Political legislation has become thoroughly unmoored from public policy scholarship and public opinion, and is now steered by lobbying and influence peddling think tanks and foundations. The post-9/11 erosion of civil liberties included, for example, the radical erosion of habeas corpus, mass government surveillance on citizens, government assassination in place of due process, and the criminalization of dissent and whistleblowing. The combination of purchased electoral politics, evacuated civil liberties, mass incarceration and disenfranchisement, a party system that principally represents the interests of big capital, and militarized domestic and foreign policies have led a number of scholars such as Wolin, Robinson, and Giroux among others to describe the United States as having slid into a proto-fascist form of government.[8]

Political theorist Chantal Mouffe offers another explanation for rising repression: the failure to recognize the political. For Mouffe, drawing on Italian Marxist Antonio Gramsci, competing blocs contest the social. Political antagonisms can be expressed through political systems that allow for difference and political resolution. Mouffe suggests that in the post-political, post-ideological era since the end of the Cold War and more recently post-9/11, political contestation and the denial of "The Political" (the constitutive friend–enemy conflict structuring the social) have resulted in a turn to antagonistic forms of extra-political expression—such as terrorism and hate crimes—aimed at annihilating the adversary as the enemy. In this view, rising repression has to do with the failure of philosophical liberalism and its recent manifestations as post-political neoliberalism to incorporate difference and contestation into the political system—a failure that a radical democracy would not suffer. Anti-immigrant, racist, and imperialist forms of nationalist violence in this view appear as the refusal of The Political and the making of the adversary into the enemy.[9] Mouffe's radical democracy offers insights into the ways that the effacement of conflict and difference in liberalism creates the conditions for fundamentalisms, including religious and market fundamentalism. This post-political denial of material and symbolic conflict has structured educational reform and has installed a logic of education as enforcement—the enforcement of the allegedly right knowledge, the denial of the cultural politics of the curriculum, the sanctification of allegedly disinterested and neutral numerical measures of truth claims that are in fact particular and partial. One of the virtues of radical democracy theory is that it recognizes that both the self and society are incomplete and constituted by difference and contestation and, hence, are always being remade by cultural work and signifying practices, that are political and pedagogical, including those in formal and informal educational institutions. Mouffe highlights the need for forms of education and cultural production that foster democratic identifications. Such democratic identifications become the basis for political and cultural participation and power sharing, as well as the basis for a collective struggle for a new radically democratic hegemony. Educators and other cultural producers are always implicated in the kinds of identifications that they affirm or contest, the kinds of subject positions they make possible for youth to occupy, and the kinds of dispositions and social relationships they foster. It is crucial to recognize the radically different patterns of identification-making for different groups of youth.

In elite schools catering to rich kids headed for positions of power in the public and private sectors, teaching is oriented around dialogue, debate, questioning, and investigation. Heavy testing, standardization, and repression foster discipline, docility, and the enforcement and transmission of knowledge—the dispositions that are encouraged for everyone else who will take subordinate roles in the economy and spectator roles in the political system. These repressive approaches to teaching aim to not only make docile workers who are expected to follow orders but they also teach everyone that the unequal distribution of power and opportunity is deserved and natural rather than being the effect of a system designed to preserve class and group privilege and exclusion. In a society theoretically committed to democracy, all schools should be teaching youth to not only engage in dialogue, debate, and questioning but also to relate knowledge to lived experience, broader social realities, and the material and symbolic contests that structure it. Repressive pedagogies succeed in isolating knowledge from the subjective and objective conditions that give rise to it. In other words, repressive pedagogies aim to prevent learning from being the basis for understanding and acting on the world. Repressive education in its variety of forms is not only part of a system of economic and political exclusion, a system for the making of anti-democratic identifications and identities, but is also a prohibition on thought.

Repressive Education and the Erasure of Thinking

While repressive forms of schooling are hardly new, I intend the expression of the *repressive social turn* in schooling to break with the history of corporal punishment, behaviorism, and Taylorism in schools. This book contends that there is something new and different about the recent rise and form of repression in public schooling. What is new, different, and ominous is not only the way that the targeting of the body for control is frequently wielded through the use of technology, surveillance, and data manipulation but also that it is interwoven with modes of teaching that render thinking, questioning, and dissent alien to the process of schooling. The chapters of this book examine different projects aimed at the bodies of students and teachers, projects that foster thoughtlessness and unthinking obedience. I share with Hannah Arendt, Erich Fromm, and Paulo Freire the contention that thinking requires estrangement of the self or dialogue with oneself.[10] That is, thinking requires a splitting—making one's experience into an object of critical analysis. The chapters in this book illustrate how numerous corporeal control projects from drugging students to biometric pedagogy, teaching "grit" (self-control), and all of the dominant educational reforms refuse to comprehend learning as thinking in this sense. Such "reforms" misframe learning as corporeal control and physiological stimulation that can be done to youth. This conception of learning as targeting the body has no place for consciousness, critical or otherwise, mediation, and reflection. In other words, as the chapters detail, these pedagogies of control are expressly aimed at denying how knowledge relates to the critical analysis of subjective experience and the broader social world. These pedagogies of control are designed to replace critical analysis that can form the basis for not only comprehending the self and society but acting to change them for a more just, equal and democratic world. Put differently, the new pedagogies of repression seek to eradicate the promise of democratic and egalitarian forms of control offered by critical education.

As Arendt insists, thinking about what we do is a precondition of ethical living. Wickedness stems from thoughtlessness. This, Arendt's well known *banality of evil* doctrine, suggests that thinking is not pure contemplation divorced from experience but rather arises from and engages lived experience. As she puts it in *Between Past and Future,* "thought itself arises out of incidents of living experience and must remain bound to them as the only guideposts by which to take its bearings."[11] Nor, for Arendt, should thinking be confused with the amassing of knowledge—the central value codified in contemporary educational policy. To think, rather, involves attention to internal dialogue, reflection on action, interpretation, and judgment. Arendt suggests that we should not try to understand evil action primarily or exclusively by seeking to locate the sadistic or malicious character or bad intent in a person. The greatest danger is unwillingness to think from the standpoint of another and to become complicit or actively involved in the destruction of the other.

In *Eichmann in Jerusalem,* Arendt, covering the trial of one of the engineers of the Holocaust, writes of Adolf Eichmann, "But the point here is that officialese became his language because he was genuinely incapable of uttering a single sentence that was not a cliché" (Arendt, 1963: 43). Arendt explains, ·

> The longer one listened to him, the more obvious it became that his inability to speak was closely connected with an inability to think, namely to think from the standpoint of somebody else. No communication was possible with him, not because he lied but because he was surrounded by the most reliable of all safeguards against the words and the presence of others, and hence against reality as such.
>
> *(44)*

Richard J. Bernstein elaborates on the deep connection between the refusal of thought and obedience to authority,

> Eichmann confirms what Arendt emphatically states. In his own handwritten notes he declares, "From my childhood, obedience was something I could not get out of my system. When I entered the armed services at the age of twenty-seven, I found being obedient

not a bit more difficult than it had been during my life to that point. It was unthinkable that I would not follow orders." He continues, "Now that I look back, I realize that a life predicated on being obedient and taking orders is a very comfortable life indeed. Living in such a way reduces to a minimum one's need to think."

(Bernstein, 286)[12]

While recent scholarship has suggested that Eichmann was not just following orders but was making decisions to actively and creatively commit genocide, Arendt was processing her own experience within a particular historical moment. Nonetheless, she makes an important contribution to philosophical and social thought as to the dangers of unthinking obedience and authoritarianism.[13] Arendt's point about the relationship between language and thinking also highlights a crucial insight of critical pedagogy about the relationship between language and power. In order to be an agent capable of acting on the world with others one needs to be able to describe, name, and develop new ways of talking about and thinking about experience and social reality that move beyond dominant discourse and the language of power that so often traps subordinate people in the values, assumptions, and clichés of ruling groups and powerful institutions. Hence, a crucial task of critical forms of education that challenge the culture of control is to provide students and teachers with a new language to describe and interpret the world as the means to understand and challenge domination and oppression and as the means to imagine and name emancipatory and egalitarian aspirations.

Arendt is hardly alone in seeing obedience and thinking at odds. Erich Fromm contends that rationality itself is based in disobedience to authority. Comparing the founding refusal, the "no" of the child to the parent to the scene in the Garden of Eden in which knowledge comes from disobeying God's prohibition, Fromm equates the possibility of autonomous thought with the individuation from godly, parental, and state authority. While Arendt suggests that thinking is ahistorical and inherently human, Fromm historically locates the development of critical consciousness with the advent of capitalism and the alienation that it makes possible. That is, the capacity of the individual to make an object of analysis out of his own life conditions, social context, and subjective experience depended, for Fromm, upon the individual's estrangement from the land, the labor process and its tools, other people, and the self.

For Fromm, as for Paulo Freire, individuals can live freely and spontaneously and act as human subjects or can opt instead to dehumanize, objectify, and instrumentalize themselves and others. Fromm and Freire share the view that to pursue freedom involves rejecting the necrophilic tendency fostered in particular by capitalism to love death and to make others and knowledge into dead static objects of control. Fromm describes the escape from freedom in the sadistic pursuit of controlling others as objects and the masochistic pursuit of solace in being controlled as an object by others. The perspectives of Fromm and Freire go far beyond critical thinking as problem solving skills. Freire elaborates on the need for individuals to objectify subjective experience, to make it into an object of analysis, to comprehend how subjectivity is formed by objective realities and forces, and for the process of theorizing experience to form the basis for a new understanding that forms the basis for agency to act on and shape the social world. The "good" objectification of knowledge and experience advocated by Freire allows individuals to comprehend the conditions of production of knowledge and experience, to analyze the economic, cultural and political struggles that inform the claims to truth made by particular groups and individuals. This stands diametrically opposed to the "bad" objectification of knowledge and experience committed for example by standardized testing and positivist forms of schooling. In standardized testing knowledge is made into an object that comes from nowhere but that must be consumed and displayed. This commodity fetishism undermines the capacity of individuals to comprehend the conditions of knowledge making, and the politics and power struggles imbuing it. The point not to be missed is that freedom comes not from rejecting any form of control. Rather, the process of learning must be understood through projects aimed at understanding and collectively and democratically controlling life conditions while ending arbitrary forms of unjustified control through which people objectify, exploit, and oppress other people.

Schooling has come to be framed as thoroughly about the accumulation of knowledge rather than thinking. Thinking is being rooted out of the school process. That which cannot be tested is seen as useless. What is at stake in the question of whether schooling fosters thinking or undermines the conditions for it is nothing short of the question of the kind of society we have. Contemporary approaches to curriculum and pedagogy are organized around the enforcement of knowledge accumulation. Not thinking. Only a society of thinking people stands a chance of making a more ethical and humane world. The call of this book then is for people to think about what they do. The chapters of this book detail how educational "innovations" are structured to prevent people from thinking about what they do. The stakes could not be higher.

The first chapter focuses on the radical expansion in prescription "smart drugs" such as Ritalin and Adderall, and the epidemic diagnosis of ADHD that coincided with the introduction of high stakes standardized testing. The chapter discusses how drugs compensate for meaningless, decontextualized learning with physiological stimulation. Smart drugs are not only a multi-billion dollar business but they are also intimately interwoven with the rise of high stakes standardized testing and a particular set of assumptions about knowledge and the self. The chapter concludes by examining the ideologies of education and intelligence expressed in mass media coverage of smart drugs in news and film.

The second chapter details the rise of "grit" pedagogy. Grit has been recently popularized by Angela Duckworth, positive psychologists at University of Pennsylvania, and *New York Times* journalist Paul Tough and has been employed by the Knowledge is Power Program (KIPP) charter school network. It was most recently taught to children by former soldiers in the UK. "Grit" is a behaviorist form of learned self-control targeting poor students of color and has been popularized post-crisis in the wake of educational privatization and defunding as the cure for poverty. Like smart drugs, grit pedagogy suggests that rather than being meaningful, learning prescribed knowledge should be endured. While smart drugs provide physiological aid in the endurance of drudgery, grit promotes cultivated habits of will. The chapter contends that grit should be understood as a neoliberal form of character education designed to suggest that individual resilience and self-reliance can overcome social violence and unsupportive social contexts in the era of the shredded social state. The chapter explains how grit pedagogy contributes to a broader ideological constellation in which education becomes a means for individualized responsibility. It concludes by contrasting the obedience-demands of neoliberal character education with the concept of social character found in the work of Erich Fromm.

The third chapter examines the rise of biometric analytic pedagogy that technology companies as well as philanthropies such as the Bill and Melinda Gates Foundation have developed and funded. The chapter begins by explaining how biometric pedagogy represents a revival of the earliest form of Taylorism that sought to routinize and control workers' bodies, and render thought the specialized domain of management. Biometric pedagogy treats students and teachers as bodies in need of measurement and control. This chapter contends that under the guise of technological sophistication and efficiency, forms of teaching are being popularized that position learning and education as passive consumer activities that do not involve thinking or the development of critical consciousness and agency. Biometric pedagogy promotes forms of motivation presumed from readings of physical stimulation rather than forms of motivation that involve dispositions of curiosity, questioning, exploration, wonder, and dialogue. This chapter contends that, despite being widely described as Orwellian experiments, biometric pedagogy shares its assumptions with the dominant educational reforms and the other repressive pedagogies detailed here.

The fourth chapter discusses corporately produced educational technologies that displace teacher control and thought. The chapter begins by highlighting the contradiction between the ideology of consumer choice that has been used to promote public school corporatization and yet has resulted in the implementation of corporate tools that undermine the choices of teachers and students. The chapter focuses on the expansion of tablet technology in the classroom promoted by News Corporation, Apple, and Microsoft and the Pearson NCS edTPA student teaching evaluation system. Promoters of tablet technology claim that their products expand teacher autonomy while I contend that they undermine it. Proponents of edTPA claim that standardizing student teaching as a videotaped performance is necessary for quality control and accountability. I contend that it treats knowledge as a commodity while displacing dialogue, thought, and critical pedagogical practice from student teaching.

The fifth chapter examines the psychopathic identifications corporations produce for subjects through their cultural pedagogical projects. It builds on the legal standing of the corporation as a person and Joel Bakan's contention in *The Corporation* that the kind of person that the corporation is happens to be a psychopath. I turn this around and ask what kind of person the corporation educates flesh and blood people to become. Examining the educational actions of education and media corporations, I discuss the recent celebration of psychopathic characters and narratives of exceptional vigilante justice. I situate these in terms of the post-9/11 political scene and social Darwinian ethos of neoliberalism. The chapter contrasts the popular TV series *Dexter* and the Ripley novels of Patricia Highsmith. While the former narratives produce authoritarian and anti-democratic identifications consistent with psychopath politics and culture, the latter represent an attempt to illustrate the impossibility of the Ayn Randian social world evacuated of conscience.

The conclusion calls for contemporary resistance against repressive education and the progressive strains of teacher unionism to be joined by a broader embrace of the traditions of critical education. I must stress that while the chapters of the book explore spectacular, sometimes extraordinary, and disturbing trends in educational practice, a crucial repeated point that I make throughout is that the assumptions about learning behind these technologies of control are not exceptional. Rather, they are the norm. What is needed, ultimately, are forms of education that comprehend claims to truth in relation to broader objective forces, structures, and struggles, as well as in relation to the making of subject positions and identifications. Rather than education being something that is enforced, education is the process of interpreting and acting on both the self and the social world towards the end of the eradication of oppressive forces, the fostering of deeply democratic social relations, and the formation of caring and egalitarian modes of associated living.

Notes

1 William I. Robinson, *Global Capitalism and the Crisis of Humanity* Cambridge: Cambridge University Press, 2014.
2 I detail the use of disaster to further otherwise unattainable rightist policy goals in education in Kenneth J. Saltman, *Capitalizing on Disaster: Taking and Breaking Schools* Boulder, CO: Paradigm, 2007.
3 Nancy Fraser, "From Discipline to Flexibilization? Rereading Foucault in the Shadow of Globalization" *Constellations* 10(2) June 2003, 160–71; David Harvey, *Seventeen Contradictions and the End of Capitalism* Oxford: Oxford University Press, 2014.
4 Luke Whelan, "Sales of ADHD Meds are Skyrocketing. Here's Why" *Mother Jones* February 24, 2015, available online at <www.motherjones.com/ environment/2015/02/hyperactive-growth-adhd-medication-sales>.
5 Preeti Upadhyaya, "How Apple, Google, Cisco are Competing for the $5 Billion K-12 Ed Tech Market" *Silicon Valley Business Journal* November 25, 2013. Available online at <www.bizjournals.com/sanjose/news/2013/11/25/heres-how-silicon-valley-will-make.html>.
6 See Slavoj Žižek *First as Tragedy, Then as Farce*, New York: Verso, 2009; Carlos Vercellone, Paul Mason, "The End of Capitalism has Begun" *The Guardian* July 17, 2015.
7 "Warren Buffett Remarks on European Debt Crisis, the "Buffett Rule" and the American Worker: Interview by Business Wire CEO Cathy Baron Tamraz" *Business Wire* November 15, 2011, available at <www.businesswire.com/news/ home/20111115006090/en/2479951/Warren-Buffett-Remarks-European-Debt-Crisis-'Buffett>.
8 See Sheldon Wolin, *Democracy, Inc.: Managed Democracy and the Specter of Inverted Totalitarianism* Princeton: Princeton University Press, 2008; William I. Robinson *Global Capitalism and the Crisis of Humanity* Cambridge: Cambridge University Press, 2014; Henry Giroux, *Against the Terror of Neoliberalism: Politics Beyond the Politics of Greed* Boulder, CO: Paradigm Publishers, 2008.
9 See most recently Chantal Mouffe, *Agonistics* London: Verso, 2014.

10 See Hannah Arendt, *The Life of the Mind* New York: Harcourt, 1978; Erich Fromm *Escape from Freedom* New York: Holt, 1941; and, Paulo Freire *Pedagogy of the Oppressed* New York: Continuum, 1972.

11 Hannah Arendt, *Between Past and Future: Six Exercises in Political Thought* New York: Viking Press, 1961, 14. Hannah Arendt, *Eichmann in Jerusalem* New York: Viking Press, 1963.

12 Richard J. Bernstein, "Arendt on Thinking" in Dana Villa (ed.) *The Cambridge Companion to Hannah Arendt* Cambridge: Cambridge University Press, 2000, pp. 277–92, 286.

13 See, for example, the debate between Richard Wolin and Seyla Benhabib in *The Jewish Review of Books* and *The New York Times* in 2014. Richard Wolin, "The Banality of Evil: The Demise of a Legend" *The Jewish Review of Books* Fall 2014, available at <http://jewishreviewofbooks.com/articles/1106/the-banality-of-evil-the-demise-of-a-legend/?print>; Seyla Benhabib, "Who's on Trial? Eichmann or Arendt?" *The New York Times* September 21, 2014, available at <http://opinionator.blogs.nytimes.com/2014/09/21/whos-on-trial-eichmann-or-anrendt/?_php=true&_type=blogs&_r=1>; Richard Wolin, "Thoughtlessness Revisited: A Response to Seyla Benhabib" *The Jewish Review of Books* September 30, 2014.

1

SMART DRUGS

Corporate Profit and Corporeal Control

ADHD, which has seen massive recent increases in diagnosis since 2000, is defined as a difficulty in paying attention, restlessness, and hyperactivity. By 2010, nearly one in three US children aged 2–17 had been diagnosed as suffering ADHD,[1] and by 2012 the diagnoses of ADHD had risen 66 percent in the prior decade.[2] Ballooning rates of diagnosis have been met with unprecedented levels of medical prescriptions, principally for the amphetamine pharmaceutical drugs Adderall and Ritalin. By 2011, 11 percent of all US children aged 4–17 were diagnosed with ADHD and 6.1 percent were taking ADHD drugs, and an estimated 8 to 35 percent of university students in the United States were using cognitive stimulants.[3] Boys are diagnosed at nearly three times the rate of girls.[4] About 80 percent of those children diagnosed with ADHD are using these medications.[5] Children below the poverty line are diagnosed at higher rates, especially poor toddlers.[6]

Some scientific literature claims that ADHD results from underdevelopment of parts of the brain responsible for executive function, that is, the parts of the brain responsible for self-control.[7] Doctors and psychologists use the US-based psychological diagnosis manual DSM-IV to diagnose ADHD 3–4 times more frequently than their European counterparts do with the ICD-10.[8] Spectacular increases in diagnosis and radically disparate rates of diagnosis lend empirical weight to cultural theories of ADHD that suggest the disorder is principally a social construct rather than a biologically based medical pathology.

As a social construct, ADHD diagnosis participates in producing and regulating social norms, drawing the boundaries for the normal and abnormal, and contributing to broader discourses about intelligence, education, and social opportunity. Usually ADHD diagnosis begins with teachers suggesting the possibility to parents. A student is restless in class, bored by lessons, and finds paying attention and sitting still excruciating. As a social construct, ADHD belies shifting social and educational values. In an era of neoliberal educational restructuring, youth are expected to display corporeal discipline, docility, and a willingness to endure lessons that are increasingly standardized, scripted, and removed from individual and social meaning. The student in the instrumentalized, hyper-rational-ized, and vocational era of neoliberal education is required to become a disciplined consumer of commodified knowledge. Proper self-discipline in the name of producing "college and career readiness" increasingly brings together the imperative for students to use the tools of bodily control to be entrepreneurial "subjects of capacity."[9] That is, proper attention is demanded of students to display test-based performance outcomes that allow the student to compete for shrinking access to the world of work, income, and commodity consumption.

Smart Drugs and the Pursuit of Profit

The steady expansion of ADHD diagnosis and cognitive stimulant pre-scription has been driven by the profit-seeking educational projects of the pharmaceutical industry.[10] The US-based industry targets parents, teach-ers, and doctors with drug advertisements and educational materials that encourage diagnosis and prescription. These educative projects have suc-ceeded. In 2010, Americans spent US$7 billion on ADHD drugs.[11] By 2015, the amount spent had risen to US$12.9 billion.[12] Clayton Pierce's biopolitical analysis emphasizes another economic dimension that he terms "extractive schooling." This refers to the ways that drugging students participates in neoliberal governmentality in which alleged educational and ultimately economic value can be extracted from the labor of teachers and students in conjunction with other neoliberal educational restructur-ing initiatives, such as value added assessment and high stakes standardized testing.

Based on an industrial efficiency model of knowledge transmission, high stakes standardized tests undermined the historical efforts of the Ele-mentary and Secondary Education Act to use federal funds progressively to support schools and districts in poverty. Instead, high stakes testing pun-ishes schools with low test scores and rewards schools with high scores, thereby exacerbating educational resource inequality by affirming the connection between the wealth of classes and the cultural capital that the tests affirm or punish.[13] In the era of neoliberal "accountability," "smart drugs" are used as a tool to raise test scores for teachers subject to value added assessment whose job security and income are now linked to test scores.[14] Likewise, in schools and districts in need of financial support and with low, stagnant, or declining test scores, smart drugs offer a means to game the regressive federal system.

The radical rise in ADHD diagnoses by two thirds over the first decade of the millennium coincided with the implementation of the federal No Child Left Behind law that centered on high stakes standardized testing. The "high stakes" part of the high stakes testing puts economic sanctions on low test scores and rewards high test scores. As Maggie Koerth-Baker has observed, "when a state passed laws punishing or rewarding schools for their standardized–test scores, ADHD diagnoses in that state would increase not long afterward. Nationwide, the rates of ADHD diagnosis increased by 22 percent in the first four years after No Child Left Behind was implemented."[15] Studies that break down ADHD diagnosis by state confirm that the states with the greatest financial penalties under No Child Left Behind are also the states with the greatest rates of diagnosis, especially for youth below the poverty line.[16]

The neoliberal imperatives for testing, scripted lessons, and direct instruction for "higher outputs" have created institutional conditions and financial rewards and punishments so that ADHD symptoms of rest-lessness, inattentiveness, and hyperactivity have become more prevalent, numerous, and more likely to be identified. That is, the new culture of control in schools is inseparable from the trend for the radical rise in the medical pathologization of students. Reasonable individual responses (like restlessness) to repressive institutional conditions—like disassociation from the environment, extreme boredom, and inability to find relevance in the assignment—have become the basis for the identification of disease and the prescription of drugs. Moreover, the medical pathologizing of students is interwoven with neoliberal ideology in education in which knowledge, learning, and intelligence are understood through the register of economic competition, social mobility, and opportunity. "From parents' and teachers' perspectives, the diagnosis is considered a success if the medication improves kids' ability to perform on tests and calms them down enough so that they're not a distraction to others."[17] As well, the high stakes testing and drugging of students facilitates the expansion of the multi-billion dollar test and textbook publishing industry, and creates profits for the medico-pharmaceutical industry. In conjunction with privatization, such as expanded chartering and its deunionizing effects, value added assessment and high stakes testing regimens participate in creating a disposable workforce of teachers who can be hired cheaply, burned out, and fired. This assures lower quality of teaching and it results in less spending on universally beneficial public goods and services.

The linkage of "smart drugs" to the precaritization of teacher work must be understood in relation to the post–2008 austerity politics that continues to promote the neoliberal pillage of the caregiving roles of the state, public schools, teacher pay, public worker jobs and pensions—all under attack as wasteful rather than as a public investment. While one might call this process "value extraction" (as Pierce does) or the disciplining of teacher work, in reality it destroys value in the process of teaching by gutting teaching experience and teacher autonomy, and displacing meaningful teaching and learning.[18] Such a trend is inextricably linked to the struggle by different classes for the use of public tax dollars to expand private control and benefit, such as school privatizations, public resource extraction and forms of education designed to make a disciplined and docile labor force or to use public tax dollars to expand public, democratic, and civic control and benefit such as the investment in public schools and the fostering of critical pedagogies that can foster a broad based struggle of democratic social relationships throughout public and private institutions. The nexus between pharmaceutical control of kids' attention and the steady expansion of standardized testing and standardization of curriculum transforms the social and individual value of knowledge while also undermining critical pedagogies and efforts to develop in students a critical consciousness for engaged social intervention. While the Every Student Succeeds Act of 2015 allows states to reduce the number of standardized tests promoted under No Child Left Behind, it maintains the requirement for standardized testing, ties state funding for teacher and leader preparation to student test scores, and comes following the federally promoted installation of a massive state-based infrastructure in testing and standardization.[19]

Smart Drugs and the Politics of Knowledge

The turn to standardized testing and to the use of "smart drugs" to increase scores is based in positivist ideology in which tested knowledge is decontextualized from the experiences of students and teachers, and delinked from its broader social significance. Positivist ideology treats knowledge as a collection of facts that are disconnected from matters of interpretation, as well as from the interests, social positions, and values of those who promote particular interpretations and claims to truth.[20] The testing trend focuses educational practice on so-called outcomes rather than on educational process. It embraces a *transmissional* model of pedagogy and curriculum in which knowledge is likened to units of commodity to be delivered, consumed, and regurgitated back on the test. Such an assumption shuts down debate, dialogue, curiosity, and creativity while making efficacy of delivery the primary focus of teaching and learning. There is clear evidence that the trends of No Child Left Behind with its outputs-based view of knowledge and tendency to shut down interpretation, debate, and creativity are experienced by students as boring and meaningless.[21]

There is a concealed politics to the positivism promoted in standardized testing. The tests obscure the interests and social power of those claiming the importance of particular knowledge while false neutrality and objectivity are promoted and assisted through the seemingly natural scientific reality of numbers. The denial of how knowledge relates to social and individual values, interests, ideologies, and experiences renders knowledge meaningful only for its abstract institutional capacity to be like economic currency or points in a game. Knowledge in this approach to teaching and learning is alienated from the social world and yet repurposed to become meaningful only for what it can gain the learner in a system of extrinsic rewards (such as grades or points) and eventually jobs, cash, and consumer goods. Put differently, what grounds the universalism of knowledge is neither its meaning to students' lives nor its meaning in the social world. The alleged universal value of knowledge on standardized tests is grounded by its abstract exchange value as currency, first in educational settings and then in economic markets. Indeed, as Theodor Adorno pointed out, the very allure of positivism is its promise of certainty and its propensity to value only that which can be numerically quantified. In this view of the social world, everything is for sale—that is, has value only for its market exchangeability.[22] Everything appears as exchange value and hence abstract. Numbers and the positivist display of quantification, Adorno points out, promise a false solidity and certainty in a world in which all things solid melt into air.

Currently, cognitive enhancement drugs are promoted as a necessity for individuals to compete in positivist forms of education so as to compete economically. As students experience decontextualized knowledge in standardized curriculum and on tests as meaningless and boring, amphetamine drugs are being used to stimulate students physically so that they can concentrate and memorize knowledge for tests. Smart drugs stimulate an artificial capacity to endure meaningless learning of decontextualized knowledge that is de-linked from students' prior experience and from the social world. The value of "stim knowledge" is its abstract exchangeability on the academic market. That is, decontextualized knowledge is recontextualized through its association as a knowledge currency, voided of its social importance other than as something with potential economic value.

Pharmacologically stimulated interest runs counter to the value that critical education places on learning that is meaningful so as to become socially and individually transformative. Put another way, drugging kids for standardized tests displaces social and political agency, the use of knowledge for students to comprehend, act on, and shape the social world they inhabit, fostering instead consumer agency in which knowledge can only be seen in terms of its exchange value for additional educational promotion but ultimately for the capacity to get money.

Smart drugs promise intelligence, but, in fact, by being promoted in conjunction with standardized testing and the standardization of curriculum, they foster ways of thinking that devalue some of the most crucial questions of knowledge and curriculum. It is crucial to emphasize that cognitive enhancers are tools. I am criticizing the use of these tools in school as compensatory for an approach to schooling that devalues thinking and abstracts knowledge from the self and society. That is, smart drugs are used to promote efficacious consumption of knowledge in place of questions that ought to be interwoven with the process of schooling such as: What values and assumptions undergird claims to truth? What are the social positions, class and cultural interests represented by knowledge and the kinds of questions that are asked? The dominant educational reforms share the same framing assumptions about knowledge as the smart drug trend.

Educational Reforms

The Common Core State Standards, the recently revised and consolidated teacher certification standards CAEP, and the new system to assess student teachers in colleges of education edTPA share crucial elements that accord with the anti-critical trends of the high stakes standardized test era and the use of smart drugs. The Common Core State Standards establish competency-based performance outcomes by grade level in language arts and mathematics. Proponents of the standards celebrate greater "rigor" defined by the implementation of "critical thinking skills" (problem solving skills) and encouragement of a Common Core of "exemplar" texts. Liberal critics of the Common Core worry that the increased standards and uneven implementation across states continue to set schools and districts up for failure and thereby continue the trend of using declarations of failure to move money out of public schools and into privatized schools like charter schools. The right-wing critics of the Common Core bemoan the loss of local autonomy and the perceived threat to the teaching of conservative values and perspectives. Critical education scholars and activists have suggested that the most significant problems with the Common Core have to do with how actual decisions about curricular content are being handed over to large for profit publishing companies such as Houghton-Mifflin, Heinemann, and Pearson NCS which make both the texts and tests for the high stakes Common Core examinations. The critical educators warn that the perceived increases in teacher autonomy under the Common Core need to be seen in terms of the continuation of a "high stakes" system of financial punishments and rewards tied to the tests. This will result in teaching to the test with the use of corporate-produced test prep and textbooks.[23] The various concerns about the Common Core and the growing opt out of testing movement put enough pressure on the Obama administration and Congress to withdraw the high stakes testing dimensions of the Elementary and Secondary Education Act in the form of the Every Student Succeeds Act. While the ESSA partially restores state and local control with regard to testing, it does not undo the expansive testing and standardization requirements and culture that dominate educational policy and practice.[24]

More pertinent to the discussion here, the standards for ESSA, the Common Core State Standards, the teacher certification standards in CAEP, and the revised guidelines for student teaching under edTPA do not encourage the comprehension of knowledge in relation to the subjective experiences, contexts, identity positions, and social conditions of students. They also do not foster forms of teaching and learning that facilitate comprehension of how subjective experience is produced by objective structures, systems, institutions, and realities in the world. They also do not encourage a critical approach to learning in which knowledge is comprehended in terms of its social conditions of production or the social conditions for acts of interpretation. They also do not treat knowledge in terms of its possibilities for facilitating political agency to reconstruct subjective experience and to engage and transform objective realities.

Smart drugs do facilitate student endurance of drudgery. The use of physical and cognitive stimulation through amphetamine can be understood with a comparison to the traditional use of coca leaf in South

America. For thousands of years, coca leaves have been chewed by rural agricultural workers to assist in enduring drudgery, the cold and damp of the Andes, and unpleasant work conditions. The dopamine and nor-epinephrine effects of both chewed coca and prescription dose levels of amphetamine, though employing different chemicals, are likewise mild pain-killers and cognitive stimulants. Similarly, caffeine, by far the most widely used cognitive stimulant on the planet, works by blocking adenosine and results in increases in multiple neurotransmitters including serotonin, dopamine, and norepinephrine. The point is that in high dosages or powerful concentrations, cognitive stimulants such as cocaine and high dose amphetamine, methamphetamine, and so on produce inebriation. While in low dose and low concentration, exemplified by coca leaf chewing and the ubiquitous coffee break, stimulants are very widely used to stanch drudgery—that is, unpleasant work. And learning knowledge that is meaningless, irrelevant, and boring is drudgery. Yet drudgery needs to be comprehended in terms of recent changes to self- and social regulation characterizing the Fordist and post-Fordist eras.

In the late 1970s and early 1980s the Fordist industrial economy gave way to post-Fordist regimes of accumulation and complementary neoliberal ideology. This shift was marked by a transition from the stable, unionized industrial economy, Keynesianism, and the compromise between labor and capital to a financially based service economy in which labor was shipped overseas and labor precarity became increasingly dominant along with neoliberal economic doctrine emphasizing monetarism, financialization, privatization, and deregulation. This shift also marked a steady decline of direct state provision of caregiving social programs to a state that would come increasingly to orchestrate and facilitate the entry of private for profit forces into public services. This shift is exemplified by the dismantling of the employment safety net in the form of welfare and its replacement by workfare, the dismantling and privatization of public housing into for profit mixed finance developments, the privatization of the military through the extensive use of mercenary contractors, the privatization of public hospitals and health services, the privatization of prisons, and the privatization of schools in the form of charters, vouchers, commercialism, contracting, and the expansion of the ideology of corporate culture to all aspects of school practice and policy.

Fordist forms of self- and social regulation involved time and labor intensive approaches to control.[25] The talking cures of psychology and psychiatry in Fordism gave way to the post-Fordist direct bodily controls of psycho-pharmacology. The prison as a place for learned rehabilitation through surveillance gave way to the prison of the locked away body (such as supermax) in which the prisoner's body is controlled with no expectation or care by authorities about rehabilitation understood as time intensive learned self-regulation.[26] The student in post-Fordism has been increasingly made into a corporate subject of these control technologies and a subject of corporeal control. Poor and working class students in post-Fordism have become subject to an increasingly carceral atmosphere in which close control of the body is paramount. This carceral control intersects with the expansion into schools of both corporate-produced security apparatus such as ID cards, metal detectors, CCTV systems, and corporately produced curriculum programs and pedagogical method-ologies such as rigid and scripted lessons, corporately managed charter schools deploying rigid prescriptive pedagogies and curriculum (KIPP and Edison Learning typify these rigid and often scripted approaches),[27] and corporately produced and administered rigid and prescriptive reme-diation methods (Supplemental Educational Services) targeting students who found the rigid and prescriptive pedagogies and curriculum pro-grams uninspiring, boring, and meaningless.

The shift from Fordism to post-Fordism revised the relationship between the state and the market. Social regulation moved away from the liberal welfare state and towards privatized and market-oriented policies with the rise of neoliberal ideology and its treatment of every social sphere as a market. The new state apparatuses in post-Fordism took increasingly privatized forms with the expansion of the privatized medical industry and the decline of public healthcare, the privatized prison, the disman-tling and privatization of public housing, and the privatized school. In post-Fordism, self-regulation for professional managerial subjects took an increasingly individualized form in the imperative for the entrepreneurial self competing in an individualized society. In this context, the hidden curriculum of Fordism, which taught all students the social relationships for the reproduction of capital, was rendered increasingly into a visible and overt curriculum. By the early 1980s public and policy discourse on public education was rapidly being remade overtly through the lens of economic interests and rationales.

Under post-Fordism, professional class students have become increas-ingly subject to corporate/corporeal controls. Educated to understand themselves primarily as entrepreneurial subjects, they learn that they must compete with the assistance of various pharmacological aids for increas-ing attention, enhancing memory, and staying awake to do school work. These pharma-discipline tools offer a medico-therapeutic legitimacy to performance enhancement. Such pharmaceutically enhanced competition is illicit and often illegal in the realm of professional sports, as witnessed by numerous Olympic, bicycling, and baseball doping scandals. Professional class students learn that they must self-administer the instruments of bodily control for educational competition towards the end of economic competition.[28]

Public Discourse on Smart Drugs

Mass media representations of both ADHD and the medical treatment of it are part of broader discourses about the social function of education, individual intelligence, and social mobility. From films to news to advertising, mass media is saturated with stories about drugs that facilitate mental adroitness, educational competition, and capitalist conquest. Yet, the public discourse on both ADHD and the overprescription of medical solutions have seldom exceeded narrow questions about the individual health side effects of putting kids on uppers and the "fairness" of using performance enhancing drugs in educational competition.[29] For example, *60 Minutes* has covered the extent to which students self-administer smart drugs to compete in school. In the *60 Minutes* segment, the only ethical issues concerning the use of amphetamine "smart drugs" such as Adderall and Ritalin are first, whether there are health consequences of putting so many kids on speed, and secondly, whether this tilts the "level playing field" for educational competition.[30] More recently, *The New York Times* has begun to publish articles on the radical overprescription of ADHD medication, staying largely with the same focus on the health and unfair competition themes.[31] In 2013, this coverage expanded to include discussion of the aggressive marketing efforts of the pharmaceutical industry in expanding the medical adoption of amphetamine smart drugs.

What is taken for granted in corporate media coverage is a system of test-oriented high stakes educational competition that filters into capitalist competition. The promise of using cognitive enhancing drugs is presented as the promise of a greater capacity to study and perform on tests, to consequently advance educationally to higher and more elite levels of schooling, and ultimately to cash educational advancement in for employment and luxury consumption of goods and services. The consumption of the drugs begins a chain of knowledge consumption that ends with rarified commodity consumption. More recent news coverage of the overprescription of Ritalin and Adderall has emphasized psychological side effects such as psychosis, withdrawal, and depression. There is more at stake in drugging kids for educational and ultimately economic competition than physical health and psychological health. The use of pharmacological technologies for educational competition participates in a broader contestation over what constitutes valuable knowledge, intelligence, and political agency. These disputes over the meaning and signs of intelligence are well illustrated in mass media by the popular Hollywood film *Limitless*.

Limitless and the Public Pedagogy of the New Intelligence

The 2011 film *Limitless* provides a compact corporate cultural pedagogy of the "smart drug." The film offers a clear illustration of the epistemological assumptions of intelligence and control in post-Fordism. Yet, it also uncritically promotes such an understanding as linked to neoliberal subject formation and a related social Darwinian sense of the social. In *Limitless*, Eddie Morra (played by Bradley Cooper) is a disheveled fiction writer with writer's block who runs into his former brother-in-law. The former brother-in-law gives Eddie a grey market designer "smart drug" called NZT, allegedly in final testing for pharmaceutical production. The drug gives Eddie vast powers of memory recall, allowing him to draw on any prior experience or text he had ever read or seen. NZT allows Eddie's mind to assemble these past experiences and texts into socially useful and meaningful information that he would immediately be able to use.

Suddenly able to recall and instantly analyze what he recalls towards clever optimized instrumental ends, Eddie writes his landlady's law review article and seduces her despite being back on the rent, writes his fiction book (on which he had missed a series of deadlines) in a few hours, and cleans his apartment (while on the drug he finds disorder and slovenliness unbearable). The more of the drug that Eddie takes, the more it turns out the intelligent use of the self is not in contemplative, creative, or culturally productive activities such as writing a novel. Rather, we learn that the intelligent drugged Eddie pursues financial speculation and wealth by borrowing money from a loan shark to gamble in the stock market, using information gleaned from corporate media investment entertainment news shows. Doubling down on his drug consumption, Eddie can absorb and synthesize vast amounts of financial data during the day while racing through the New York party scene at night and globally jet-setting on the weekend. Intelligent activity is speculative finance (gambling in casino capitalism) and hyper-consumption.

As side effects such as amnesia kick in, top investors take notice of Eddie's sudden wealth as do loan sharks and mobsters who want the smart drug too. Surviving assassination, murder frame up, and the sickness from withdrawal, Eddie then moves to the next logical scene of hyper-intelligence: US electoral politics. He has secured his own production of clean NZT, so his senate bid will clearly be a stepping stone to the presidency. In the film, intelligence is defined through the positivist assumption of an accumulation of facts and sense-data. The facts do not just speak for themselves but they assemble themselves into valuable knowledge for the individual actor. When one takes NZT, one does not think in the sense of contemplation, reflection, or mediation. The thinking in the form of data accumulation is so fast that it collapses into pure action.

Limitless offers not just a view of intelligence that accords with positivist rationality but presents a blunt equivalency between intelligence and the most conservative pursuits and behaviors. Creative writing that might question the social order and that requires reflection and the work of thinking and imagining is discarded in favor of turning the self into a data processing machine for stock market gambling. Politics is presented as the next stage in self-promotional power-seeking behavior. This framing of what it means to engage the political adopts a neoliberal view of politics as an extension of corporate management or venture capital typified by neoliberal politicians.

In his book *The Soul at Work,* Franco Berardi explains that panic and anxiety are intensified by information technologies that temporally accelerate the flow of information to the subject at an infinite rate while the body has a finite biological limit with which to interpret and assemble the information.[32] Of course, the widespread use and abuse of anti-anxiety benzodiazepine drugs such as Valium and Xanax mitigate the emotional experience of the acceleration imperative in the realms of work, school, and consumption. The imagined drug of *Limitless,* NZT, is a mirror reflection of Xanax or Valium, the anti-anxiety hypnotic which stands as the most abused pharmaceutical. Rather than slowing the subject to emotionally cope with informational acceleration as benzodiazepines do, NZT speeds up the capacity of the subject for apperception of sense data. It expands the biological limit with which to interpret and assemble information. This gives the user a feeling of confidence, control, and impatience—the need to move forward to maintain the high flow of informational consumption. Technologically, the analogue to this is Internet or smart phone "addiction" in which the subject feels anxiety about not being subject to the fast flow of information, not plugged in, wired. The real world pharmacological analogue to NZT is Adderall and Ritalin, what used to be called "speed" and are today's dominant smart drugs. In the 1970s and 1980s, these same amphetamines were widely prescribed to curb consumption of food. Now these amphetamines are widely overprescribed to facilitate the consumption of information that is individually meaningless but valuable for educational competition and promotion towards the end of economic competition.

The American Academy of Pediatricians warns parents to keep children under the age of two away from all screens.[33] According to medicine there are no developmental benefits for infants from watching TV or computers. In part, this is because babies need to contemplate and then seek to interact with objects and images in the world. Screen time functions as a kind of hypnotic offering intense visual stimuli but disallowing contemplative engagement with the object. While correlations between excessive early-age screen time for children and the onset of ADHD are established in medical literature, the epidemic has to be investigated in terms of how these dynamics stunt development for contemplative engagement with the object. There is a simple explanation for why ADHD drugs are effective for those who have been exposed to excessive screen time from an early age. What is on the screen is more physiologically stimulating than reality. Stimulant drugs add physiological excitation to a reality that appears mundane as a consequence of habituated screen stimulation. ADHD drugs temporarily restore to mundane reality the physiologically stimulation provided early on by the fast cuts and flickering images of bodies and explosions. This explanation would seem to be backed by recent studies of cell phone usage that indicate that people get physiologically addicted to checking email and texts.[34] Each checking of a message on the phone results in a little squirt of the body's natural pain killer dopamine. Not even getting a new message but simply checking the message inbox causes the release of the body's natural painkillers.

The medical remedy for ADHD is speed, Adderall or Ritalin, which functions like the fictional NZT of *Limitless* to bring the subject "up to speed" and which restores the capacity for concentration/attention lost through early and heavy exposure to the passive stimulation of flickering screens. NZT differs in that it removes contemplation from the equation and allows one to have thinking happen to one automatically. This should be seen then as the dream of corporate ideology. Thought is replaced by stimulation. As Chapter 3 on biometrics details, this dream of corporate ideology of displacing thought and mediation with physiological stimulation is being promoted by technology companies encouraged by corporate philanthropies. The media stimulation of advertising driven screen content in children produces a mental habit of externally driven excitation that simultaneously renders non-media experience as slow, drab, and inert (*Limitless* illustrates the drab unstimulated state Eddie experiences prior to NZT). Smart drugs such as Adderall and Ritalin restore physiological stimulation lost through the absence of screens, that is, they restore media stimulated consciousness. As such, they overcome "attention deficit" by allowing boring, meaningless, and decontextualized forms of learning to be, if not interesting, then endurable.

Smart drugs used in conjunction with repressive pedagogies hence have a political implication that is diametrically opposed to that of critical pedagogy. Critical pedagogy addresses experiences which are meaningful to students and helps them to comprehend those meaningful experiences in terms of the broader forces and struggles that produce those experiences. Smart drugs are being overprescribed in order to work on the body to allow the mind to endure or even enjoy the focus on that which is meaningless so that students can study for standardized tests and their decontextualized content. This corporate dream of replacing thought with stimulation is the same dream promoted by the public pedagogy of the film and in fact it is the same dream of ending contemplative thought that animates the positivist school reforms of standardized testing, scripted lessons and the rest. Contemplative thought, the work of interpretation, cedes to the memorization and accumulation of decontextualized facts. In *Limitless,* intelligence is the mind's automatic meaning-making activities that require no conscious thought. Intelligence happens behind one's back as a pharmacological effect. In contemporary positivist school reforms such as standardized testing, the meanings behind the facts, the selection and value of truth claims are determined elsewhere by the ones who know, the experts, the test makers who sit in the offices of large corporations such as Educational Testing Services and Pearson NCS. Thought resides there, with them. The practice of drugging children for test preparation undermines intelligence, the work of interpretation and judgment of the meanings of texts and claims to truth.

Critical pedagogies ideally begin with meaningful student experience and educative contexts to foster interpretation of how broader social forces produce these contexts and meaningful experiences. Such interpretation ideally forms the basis for social intervention. While critical pedagogies aim to expand understanding of the production of both knowledge and subjective experience, prescriptive methodologies and positivist forms of schooling aim to decontextualize knowledge and reduce comprehension of experience to the individual. The contemporary discourse and use of smart drugs contributes to conceptions of the self, the social, and the school that are at odds with public and critical forms of schooling and life.

Notes

1 National Survey of Children with Special Health Care Needs, available at <http://childhealthdata.org/browse/survey/results?q=1954>.
2 Science Daily <www.sciencedaily.com/releases/2012/03/120319134214. htm>.
3 Kimberly Holland and Elsbeth Riley, "ADHD by the Numbers" Healthline, available at <www.healthline.com/health/adhd/facts-statistics-infographic#1>.
4 Ibid.
5 Alan Schwarz and Sarah Cohen, "A.D.H.D. seen in 11% of US Children as Diagnoses Rise" *The New York Times* March 31, 2013, available at <www.nytimes.com>. Alan Schwarz, "Attention-Deficit Drugs Face New Campus Rules" *The New York Times*, April 30, 2013. See also the National Survey of Children with Special Health Care Needs, available at <http://childhealthdata.org/browse/survey/results?q=1840>.
6 Alan Schwarz, "Thousands of Toddlers are Medicated for ADHD Report Finds, Raising Worries" *The New York Times* May 16, 2014, A11.
7 These scientific explanations suggest that how these parts of the brain use dopamine may explain the reduced executive function.
8 Ilina Singh, "Beyond Polemics: Science and Ethics of ADHD." *Nature Reviews. Neuroscience* 9(12) (December 2008), 957–64.
9 See Nancy Fraser's discussion of neoliberal forms of self-regulation in "From Discipline to Flexibilization?" See also Angela McRobbie's "Top Girls? Young Women and the Post-Feminist Sexual Contract" *Cultural Studies* 21(4–5) (2007), 718–37. McRobbie provides the concept of neoliberal "subjects of capacity."
10 Clayton Pierce, *Education in the Age of Biocapitalism* New York: Palgrave Macmillan, 2013.
11 Brendan L. Smith, "Inappropriate Prescribing" *Monitor on Psychology* 43(6) (June 2012), 36, available at <www.apa.org/monitor/2012/06/prescribing.aspx>.
12 Luke Whelan, "Sales of ADHD Meds are Skyrocketing. Here's Why" *Mother Jones* February 24, 2015, available at <www.motherjones.com/environment/2015/02/hyperactive-growth-adhd-medication-sales>.
13 This issue of the relationship between cultural capital and high stakes testing is taken up at greater length in Kenneth Saltman, *The Failure of Corporate School Reform* Boulder, CO: Paradigm, 2012. See Pierre Bourdieu "The Forms of Capital" and Bourdieu and Passeron, "Social and Cultural Reproduction in Education."

14 Value added assessment measures teachers' value by their students' standardized test score changes. It seeks to transform teacher labor by undermining tenure, security, unions, and teaching experience, instead linking test score outputs to bonus pay. The practice of evaluating teachers based on their students' test scores leads to insecure employment. See Mark Garrison, *A Measure of Failure: The Political Origins of Standardized Testing* Albany: SUNY Press, 2009; and Mark Garrison, "Value-Added Measures and the Rise of Anti-Public Schooling," in *The Phenomenon of Obama and the Agenda for Education* Charlotte, NC: Information Age Publishers, 2014.

15 Maggie Koerth-Baker, "The Not-So-Hidden Cause behind the A.D.H.D. Epidemic" *The New York Times* October 15, 2013.

16 Caroline Miller, "The Truth About ADHD: Over-Diagnosis Linked to Cause Championed by Michelle Rhee" Salon.com March 1, 2014, available at <www.salon.com/2014/03/01/the_truth_about_adhd_over_diagnosis_linked_to_cause_championed_by_michelle_rhee/>.

17 Koerth-Baker, "The Not-So-Hidden Cause behind the A.D.H.D. Epidemic."

18 See Clayton Pierce, *Education in the Age of Biocapitalism* for the position that value added assessment and the use of smart drugs are aimed at extraction of economic value.

19 Alia Wong, "The Bloated Rhetoric of No Child Left Behind's Demise" The Atlantic December 9, 2015, available at <www.theatlantic.com/education/archive/2015/12/the-bloated-rhetoric-of-no-child-left-behinds-demise/419688/>.

20 On the ideology and culture of positivism in education see Henry Giroux's *Theory and Resistance in Education* Westport: Bergin and Garvey, 1983.

21 HSSSE High School Survey of Student Engagement, see <http://ceep.indiana.edu/hssse/images/HSSSE_2010_Report.pdf>.

22 See Theodor Adorno, *Introduction to Sociology* Stanford: Stanford University Press, 2000.

23 See Rethinkingschools.org "Editorial: The Trouble with the Common Core" 27(4) Summer 2013, available at <www.rethinkingschools.org>.

24 Alia Wong, "The Bloated Rhetoric of No Child Left Behind's Demise."

25 See Fraser "From Discipline to Flexibilization?"

26 See Michel Foucault's elaboration on the panopticon and the expansion of the technology of surveillance in education and other fields in *Discipline and Punish*. On the argument that learned self-regulation has been partly displaced by direct control of bodies see Gilles Deleuze's essay "Societies of Control," *L'autre Journal* 1 (1990); Zygmunt Bauman, *Globalization: The Human Consequences* New York: Polity, 2000; David Garland, *The Culture of Control,* and Fraser "From Discipline to Flexibilization?"

27 For details and a textual analysis of the rigid Success for All reading pedagogy see Kenneth J. Saltman, *The Edison Schools* New York: Routledge, 2005. Diane Ravitch celebrates the rigid approach of KIPP in *The Death and Life of the Great American School*. Here she admires the firm handshake and steady eye contact demanded of poor minority students suggesting that such forms of physical control are the ticket to economic inclusion and academic success. Repeating a colonial educational trope and consistent with her nostalgia for pre-civil rights public education, this affirmation of corporeal coercion should be seen

as centrally related to Ravitch's neoconservative view of culture that demands assimilation to a Eurocentric and conservative canon held to be of universal value and that allegedly represents the interests and histories of everyone. At the core of such approaches is submission and docility to powerful groups and institutions and their traditions rather than education as a practice of freedom and dissent in the critical pedagogical tradition.

28 See Joel Bakan, *Childhood Under Siege* New York: Free Press, 2011. The current rampant uses of pharmacology to self-administer educational competition dosing can be found in a *60 Minutes* segment "Boosting Brain Power" April 25, 2010, available at <www.cbsnews.com/video/watch/?id=6430949n&tag=contentBody;storyMediaBox>.

29 Such dominant concerns about ADHD and the self-administration of smart drugs for educational and economic competition are typified by a *60 Minutes* segment "Boosting Brain Power" April 25, 2010.

30 "Boosting Brain Power" *60 Minutes* April 25, 2010.

31 See for example, Schwarz and Cohen, "A.D.H.D. seen in 11% of US Children as Diagnoses Rise."

32 See Franco Berardi, *The Soul at Work* New York: Semiotext(e), 2009.

33 American Academy of Pediatrics "Media Use by Children Younger than 2 Years" *Pediatrics* 128(5) (November 2011), 1040–5, available at: <http://pediatrics.aappublications.org/content/128/5/1040>.

34 See Matt Richtel, *A Deadly Wandering: A Tale of Tragedy and Redemption in the Age of Attention* New York: HarperCollins, 2014, which in the context of explaining why texting while driving is so dangerous provides a comprehensive recent overview of the scientific literature on the physiological and attentional effects of texting and other screen usage. Richtel does not, however, address attention in the context of learning. On the neuroscience of attention see, for example, the work of Adam Gazzaley, David L. Strayer, and Daphne Bavelier. Unfortunately, these researchers tend to share assumptions about learning that this book is criticizing.

2

THE AUSTERITY SCHOOL

Grit, Character, and the Privatization of Public Education

Introduction

Since the 2008 financial crisis, the politics of austerity have centrally involved amplifying the longstanding neoliberal program of gutting the caregiving roles of the state while expanding privatization and deregulation. As David Harvey suggests, neoliberalism has, since the economic crisis of the 1970s, been used by the capitalist class to legitimize draconian policies that restore and consolidate class power by privatizing profit while socializing risk and eroding the power of workers and unions under the guise of fiscal discipline.[1] Public education in the United States has been one of the caregiving institutions subject to a steadily increasing neoliberal fiscal starvation, privatization, and deregulation.[2]

Austerity politics informs the structural dimensions of education, such as funding and finance, including a post-2008 intensification of the steady expansion of school privatizations in the form of charters, vouchers, scholarship tax credits (tax subsidies for private schools that drain the tax base for public schools), and union-busting, as public money is siphoned away from children and towards investor profits and business slush funds.[3] Facilitated by the growing charter movement, the closure of public schools represents a corporate hijacking of the US public school system. It installs, in neighborhood schools, a system of contracting out and a low-paid, insecure, and inexperienced teacher workforce.[4]

Austerity politics has also included an amplification of a three decade long radical remaking of the culture of education by applying the language and logic of business to school culture, district administration, curriculum, and pedagogy. Educational accountability imagined through the lens of fiscal discipline has involved expanding market ideals of competition for scarce resources and consumer choice. This has resulted in naming of superintendents "CEO," justifying privatizations by modeling districts on stock portfolios, launching Wall Street style shell games with test scores, implementing regressive funding formulas typified by "high stakes testing" that replace equity-based Title I funding for poor schools through funding cuts, and ceding policy governance to super-rich individuals and philanthropic foundations intent on applying private sector schemes to states, districts, schools, and students.[5] As many critics have argued, the social cost of neoliberal educational restructuring is the humanistic, social, civic engagement, and critical pedagogical possibilities of public education. Instead, schooling is justified through reference to vocationalism, economic instrumentalism, and transmission-oriented approaches to knowledge and learning that do not examine how claims to truth relate to broader material and symbolic contests.[6] These ideological trends are interwoven with the multi-billion dollar bonanza in standardized test and textbook publishing tied to high stakes standardized testing and the standardization of curriculum typified by No Child Left Behind, the Common Core State Curriculum Standards, and their corporate beneficiaries such as Pearson NCS, Houghton-Mifflin, McGraw-Hill, Heinemann, ETS, News Corp and others. Austerity education also sees the newfound embrace of a culture of control in classrooms and direct control over working class and poor students' bodies. These range from narrow corporeal imperatives— such as feet on the floor, hands on the desk, eyes tracking the teacher—and biometric devices, to behaviorist cues, scripted lessons, standardization of space and time, and the modeling of entire schools on the prison and military.[7] In 2015 grit became more deeply institutionalized in educational policy. Data collection on grit was incorporated into the NAEP federal test "The Nation's Report Card" and the Every Student Succeeds Act that replaced No Child Left Behind federally funds questionable measures of grit and other social emotional learning as partial alternatives to measure teacher efficacy.[8]

Privatized school management typified by the charter school movement and its venture philanthropy backers is responsible for the promotion of "scaling up" homogeneous school models that are characterized by a climate of repressive control in schools.[9] The largest for profit education company, EdisonLearning, and the largest private charter manager, KIPP, both of which target working class and poor schools for management, exemplify corporate models of austerity thinking in the classroom. They impose highly standardized curricula, tight controls over teacher and student behavior with scripted lessons, the teaching of the same lessons in all schools at the same time, centralized data-tracking of numerical test measures, value-added assessments that measure teacher and teacher educator performance based on student test scores over time, and rewarding success in these measurements over teacher experience, further education, and career security. That is, in the age of austerity, subjects are formed through repressive pedagogies. Punitive disciplinary practices and policies including hierarchical surveillance, security apparatus, militarization, and punishment control and coerce working class and poor students.[10] A number of scholars, myself included, in the past twenty years have understood such expanded repressive control as part of the broader economic and cultural market fundamentalism that rolls back social investment, support, and care and rolls out new investment in punishment, containment, and coercion, making youth into commodities in the exploding industries of for profit education.[11]

In what follows here, I first further explain austerity education as both a continuation and intensification of longstanding neoliberal restructuring of public schooling by situating it in terms of the insights of social and cultural reproduction theory that highlights how schools reproduce the social relations for the reproduction of capital.[12] Despite its limitations, reproduction theory is important to recover as one lens to comprehend how schoolkids, an increasingly disposable labor force in the making, become the means through which capital can be reproduced in the short term and why, in the era of austerity, most direct forms of repression take such a prominent place in the newest incarnations of public school "reform."[13] The second section delves more deeply into one manifestation of the growing culture of repression in schools by focusing on the recent austerity-era popularization of "grit." "Grit" is a pedagogy of control that is predicated upon a promise made to poor children that if they learn the tools of self-control and learn to endure drudgery, then they can compete with rich children for scarce economic resources. Proponents of teaching "grit" contend that the poor are biologically and psychologically traumatized by poverty. The trauma of poverty, they argue, can be overcome through learned self-control and submission to authority within the school. "Grit," proponents allege, is a new apolitical form of character education in which becoming educated is explained through instrumentalism, efficiencies, and above all submission to authority. My contention here is that "grit" continues the longstanding political project of the right to not merely individualize responsibility for social conditions and life chances but to emphasize promises of subjective control and agency in which the individual's body and mind become loci of control in the service of what Giroux has discussed as "the disimagination machine":

> The "disimagination machine" is both a set of cultural apparatuses extending from schools and mainstream media to the new sites of screen culture, and a public pedagogy that functions primarily to undermine the ability of individuals to think critically, imagine the unimaginable, and engage in thoughtful and critical dialogue. Put simply, to become critically informed citizens of the world.[14]

That is, grit actively produces knowledge, forms of selfhood, and political affiliation at odds with self and social criticism and reflection that can form the basis for interpretation and intervention. I finish by contrasting "grit" with Erich Fromm's diametrically opposite concept of "social character" that emphasizes how the development of rationality is founded in disobedience to authority and a dialectical conception of the self that is socially formed and inevitably imbricated in making society.

Education in Austerity

Since 2008, austerity politics has included simultaneously defunding and privatizing public education while scapegoating it for economic conditions not of its own making. The recent popularization of targeting poor students to learn "grit" represents in part the embrace across the political spectrum of what had been an educational slogan on the political right: "methods not money." The defunding and privatization of public education that has continued since the Reagan administration goes hand in hand with the push to scapegoat teachers and students, blaming them for outcomes caused by radically disparate educational and social investments. Teacher bashing has reached unprecedented levels as a steady message of school failure and teacher blame is relentlessly promoted in mass media. Taking the lead from right-wing think-tank ideologues such as Eric Hanushek, the neoliberal venture philanthropy the Bill and Melinda Gates Foundation poured money into promoting the idea that the individual teacher is the single most important factor responsible for raising standardized test scores. For members of the professional class benefitting from massive investment in public schools in rich communities, this was of course reassuring. After all, if only individual teacher behavior matters, then redistributive schemes to equalize the sometimes one to three spending differences between schools in poor and rich areas, respectively, are futile and do nothing, they say, but sacrifice "excellence."[15]

President Obama, former Chair of the Federal Reserve Ben Bernanke, and *New York Times* columnist Thomas L. Friedman each responded to the massive job loss by suggesting that if only teachers were doing their jobs then the unemployment crisis would be solved.[16] The films *Waiting for Superman, The Lottery,* and *The Cartel* were joined by NBC TV and countless news items conveying the message that public schooling has failed, individual teachers are largely responsible, and the only solution is the radical embrace of market-based experiments, especially chartering. This media blitz incidentally coincided with clear educational policy research for the failure of market-based reforms to do what proponents had promised all along—namely, raise standardized test scores.[17]

The popularizing of "grit" in 2012 was significant for marking a shift towards a reinvigorated scapegoating of students for conditions not of their making in addition to the ongoing assault on teachers, public workers and their unions, and secure employment. The new turn to teaching grit has to be understood, as well, as part of a significant shift in the working of social and cultural reproduction that involves making the social relations for the reproduction of capital.

Reviving Reproduction Theory for the Age of Austerity

In the last two decades, neoliberals have succeeded in radically changing the traditional two-tiered educational system into a new two-tiered educational system. Scholars of educational reproduction have long explained how schools reproduce the racialized class hierarchy not only by teaching students of different class positions the skills and know-how for work.[18] Reproduction theorists also explain that different emphases on skills and know-how come wrapped in ideologies of knowledge and social relations crucial for the reproduction of relations of production and their subjectivities.

In the era of industrial production, the US public school system largely prepared professional class students for leadership and managerial roles in the private and public sectors while preparing working class and poor students for wage manufacturing labor.[19] Professional class schools prepared students for advanced university education while fostering dispositions of curiosity, dialogue, and debate within acceptable ideological frameworks. Working class schools largely prepared students with basic skills and dispositions for obedience to authority, an alignment of knowledge with expert authority, and internalized blame for limited educational and work advancement.[20] Sorting and sifting mechanisms—such as grades, testing, and tracking—naturalized and legitimated, as matters of talent or merit, unequal distribution of life chances and reproduction theorists described this ideological magic as the "hidden curriculum." (As these theorists also recognized, this ideological work was much more complicated, contradictory, and interwoven with other ideologies, including nation, gender, sexuality, race.) What was "hidden" in the hidden curriculum was the capitalist basis for the organization of time and space, the practices of teaching and learning that assured an adequate supply of both mandarins for those who owned the society and the exploitable reserve army of labor whose time and labor power could be captured and accumulated as profit by owners. But what happens to this arrangement when capitalist accumulation no longer needs the workers at the bottom?

Since the early 1970s, deindustrialization, the shift to the service economy, advances in computer and transportation technologies, trade and capital deregulation, steady increases in worker productivity combined with steadily declining real wages have resulted in a debt and speculation economy and a series of bubbles that popped—stock, dot-com, mortgage-backed security. By the 1990s, the productive manufacturing economy steadily declined as a source of corporate profits while speculation as the basis for corporate wealth steadily surpassed it.[21] As Richard Wolff has argued, the decline of wages coupled with upward worker productivity resulted in a situation in which expanded consumption and economic growth could be accomplished by corporations lending unpaid wages back to workers in the form of credit cards, home equity loans, student loans, and car loans.[22] Corporate profits skyrocketed as unpaid wages were returned with interest obligations and corporations awash in cash needed new venues for profitable investment. As the speculative economy overtook the productive economy in the mid-1990s, corporations, flush from decades of upward redistribution, discovered public education as an US$800 billion a year "industry" ripe for the taking.[23] As profit has become tougher to extract in the private sector, corporations and investors look to seize portions of the public sector, through lucrative contracts in for profit school management and a vast array of educational products and services. The profit made by investors drains public resources that would otherwise be spent on educational services. The standardized testing push of the 2000s was interwoven with the financial interests of test makers and textbook publishers, curriculum producers, and contracting companies, including technology firms. The standardization of knowledge through standardized testing and standardization of curriculum lends itself to the financial pursuits of market fundamentalists who want to treat knowledge as an industrial commodity and use private sector methods for "delivery," measurement, and control.

The new two-tiered system involves a revised social and cultural reproduction in schools. If the public schools in the industrial era provided a dual labor force for a dual economy, public schools in the post-industrial era can be seen as making a dual labor force for a different kind of dual economy. As Nancy Fraser argues, the era of neoliberal globalization results in a new dual mode of social and self-regulation.[24] While in the industrial era, control took the predominant form of learned self-regulation, in the post-industrial economy, learned self-regulation gives way to more direct control of the body.

In working class public schools, the models of the military and the prison, and old behaviorist and scientific management ideals of controlling bodies are revived and applied to working class kids. For example, KIPP charter school management company, which is one of the largest and most celebrated and promotes teaching grit, also employs a behaviorist model of body control called SLANT, which is an acronym for Sit straight, Listen, Ask a question, Nod your head, Track. Infractions against the behavior code result in being ordered to stand for long periods of time on a black line in the hallway and getting demerit points in a book that is referred to as "the paycheck." A common student nickname for KIPP which stands for "Knowledge is Power Program" is Kids in Prison Program.

More broadly urban, poor, and predominantly non-White schools receive a heavy police presence, metal detectors, biometric ID cards, strict dress codes, strict codes of behavior punishable with not just expulsion but arrest. With the rise of school funding linked to test scores, an epidemic has emerged: drugging kids into attention and out of distracting other kids has been driven by desperate attempts to control the bodies of children in order to game the standardized tests and assure federal funding.[25]

Meanwhile, professional class youth are being educated to use the instruments of corporeal self-control to make themselves into allegedly entrepreneurial subjects of capacity. In this case, as I discuss in the prior chapter, students learn that they ought to use smart drugs such as Adderall, Ritalin, Concerta and other amphetamine stimulants to facilitate attention to compete against others. These more direct forms of corporeal control do not replace but supplement the more characteristically industrial era uses of disciplinary power.[26]

The new social and cultural reproduction creates social relations for the reproduction of capital in education in part by producing a more intensely disciplined future labor force. As Bertell Ollman argues, with the advent of the flexible labor force, the conditions of neoliberal globalization, new pressures on workers, and the pillaging of public schools by businesses, the radical expansion of standardization and standardized testing plays a crucial reproductive role of teaching students the new not-so-hidden curriculum of schooling for capitalism.[27] The emphasis on student discipline and docility through the enforcement of standardized regimes reveals what Ollman calls the real lessons of testing: obeying authority, understanding truth to reside with those in power, and preparing for work speed-ups. Such discipline becomes crucial in the context of a steadily worsening economy in the United States as factories—and with them unionized and secure jobs—have been shipped overseas in the past few decades under the economic dictates of neoliberalism. In the industrial era, the time and labor intensive making of future workers for their exploitable labor gives way to the postindustrial pillage of public services for short term profits. What matters is controlling bodies and extracting profit in the short run from those bodies. The new repression in schools is expedient not only for catering to the expansion of the growing low-skill, low-paid workforce of the future. The new repression crucially facilitates immediate profit-taking in education through for profit school management contracts, mandated testing, and corporate monopolies for test and text production, real estate deals facilitated through chartering, for profit remediation services, and the security industries. Moreover, as the private sector continues to pillage public education, private sector metrics of quality and value have become the dominant mode for describing school.

Not only have knowledge and learning been subject to being quantifiably measured and declared neutral objects for efficient delivery. Also, all of the new educational reforms—from Common Core curriculum standards to No Child Left Behind, Race to the Top, the revised standards for teacher certification CAEP, the revised students teaching standards edTPA—treat knowledge as needing to be delinked from both student experience and broader social, cultural, political, and economic forces and struggles. Knowledge in this view is meaningful only for its abstract value delinked from how people subjectively interpret it or how it contributes to an understanding and transformation of the objective world. These reforms frame knowledge as meaningful only for its exchange value.

It is evacuated of its humanistic aims of individual edification and political value for civic participation and collective self-governance. Standardization has been used by neoliberal reformers in the name of educational efficiencies to wage war on any form of education that would explain the individual and social contexts in which knowledge becomes meaningful. Knowledge in this view is not understood as being produced through unequal dialogic exchange or being the outcome of struggles. Instead, knowledge is something to enforce.[28]

Grit

In the new culture of austerity, the disciplinary mechanism is often the student herself. That is, as neoliberal economic reforms promise a withdrawal of the caregiving arm of the state, schools work to privatize responsibility. Making the draconian disciplinary apparatus of the neoliberal age invisible, these schools also make it seem like individuals, rather than social supports and public investments, are failing. A number of scholars, journalists, education reformers, and charter school proponents have recently popularized the concept of "grit" in US educational reform policy to refer to this individualization of educational effort.[29] "Grit" refers to "self-discipline wedded to a dedicated pursuit of a goal."[30] The most publicized proponents commonly define grit as the dedicated pursuit of a passion such as mastering a musical instrument. Yet the "grit scale" that measures grit makes no distinction between intrinsic motivation for a goal and capacity to pursue something that has no inherent meaning to the pursuer.[31] Proponents have identified grit as a developmental character trait that is responsible for academic and work "success" defined by sustained motivation towards the end of task completion. Grit-oriented pedagogies aim to instill rule following in children. Such pedagogies seek to structure the school environment to remove activities that are not purposive and instrumental, precluding activities oriented around exploration, play, and imagination.[32] Grit-oriented forms of pedagogy involve heavy doses of corporeal control, physical cues, and rapid-fire shallow exchanges between teachers and students that are geared towards eliciting "right" answers rather than towards thoughtful dialogue.

The popularization of grit relies upon a few key assumptions and fallacies about learning, knowledge, and intelligence. Among these is the assumption that mastery of skills and knowledge can be boiled down to putting in enough hours of what grit proponent Angela Duckworth calls "deliberate practice." Duckworth suggests that if everyone (especially kids) learned better self-control, delayed gratification, and goal-setting, more skills and talent would be fostered and individuals would live more fulfilled lives, becoming more successful and excellent at what they pursue; and the economy would benefit.

Grit enthusiasts claim that grit marks a move away from seeing the student as needing to be filled with knowledge in the empiricist tradition. Yet, because the discourse on grit denies cultural politics of knowledge and embraces standardized testing, it remains committed to a conception of learning that Paulo Freire referred to as "banking education." In "banking education" as Freire describes it, students are empty vessels to be filled with the right knowledge.[33] To this old empiricist conception of education, grit adds a renewed onus on the learner to develop the will and disposition to get filled up.[34] Grit revives the Kantian educational emphasis on learned self-discipline but with the moral and public uses of education stripped out.[35] It also revives the Aristotelian virtue ethics emphasis on character education but with the moral and political dimensions replaced by narrow training and economic justifications.[36]

While character education in the West can be traced back to Aristotle's *Nicomachean Ethics*, its contemporary revival in education harkens back to cultural conservative efforts in the 1980s culture wars to link character development to civic participation. As called for by figures such as E. D. Hirsh, William Bennett, and Allen Bloom, this participation depends upon elite, Eurocentric, and canonical knowledge. Cultural conservatives elevated character education for a deontological ethics posited against the threat of cultural relativism that multiculturalism and its valuation of cultural difference were posing. Then in the 1990s, perhaps in response to a presidency defined by allegations of personal immoral conduct, the Democratic Clinton administration further promoted character education, aligning individual moral development with the public good and the values of civic life. Of course the Clinton administration made its defining policies the dismantling and gutting of the caregiving roles of the state (like replacing welfare with workfare) while deregulating markets and undermining collective forms of security. In this context an emphasis on individualized responsibility shared much with the contemporary promotion of grit. However, today's emphasis on character education—or "grit"—in the age of austerity marks a radical break with prior conceptions animated by ethical and political ideals. Rather, grit is a strictly economic self-regulatory ideal understood through personal efficiency and productivity. This conception of character accords with the trend of neoliberal educational restructuring in which schooling is seen as a tool promoting national business competition and individual competition for increasingly scarce economic mobility on a global scale.

In his book popularizing grit, *How Children Succeed: Grit, Curiosity, and the Hidden Power of Character*, *New York Times* journalist Paul Tough explains grit as a new apolitical and amoral form of character education. Character in Tough's view involves the disposition to persist in doing what one does not find meaningful or motivating. The poor, according to Tough, ought to learn to endure drudgery at an early age because endurance of drudgery is a better indicator of both academic and work success as measured, respectively, by grades and earnings.[37]

The narrative about grit naturalizes poverty and inequality by drawing on biological studies and by stitching them to a neoliberal social Darwinian perspective on the naturalness of markets and individual competition. While some people are alleged to have more grit than others naturally, the rich are alleged to have more grit as a result of supportive environmental conditions that the poor do not have. This is where the alleged "science" of grit comes to it. Rich children are alleged to have better "executive function" than poor children. That is, they are supposed to be able to voluntarily regulate their behavior to a greater degree. Tough explains that stressed poor children (just like stressed lab rats) have less memory (which Tough equates with intelligence) than unstressed children. Likewise, Tough explains that the "incentive processing system" and "cognitive control system" which develop especially in adolescence are compromised by the "high allostatic load" (stress) of living in poverty. In Tough's narrative, if students could be taught self-control and goal-setting, then they could properly channel their stress towards self-control and discipline for "academic achievement;" that is, decontextualized learning and later inclusion into the workforce. Tough and the other proponents of grit are especially enthusiastic about addressing the stress of poverty not by reducing or ending poverty and all of its violence but by teaching children to channel the stress produced by poverty so that they learn how to endure drudgery for potential opportunity in capitalist labor markets.

Tough draws on neoliberal economist James Heckman to claim that grit, more than intelligence or creativity, results in economic mobility and opportunity regardless of class origin. Yet, as Thomas Piketty's *Capital in the Twenty-First Century* empirically illustrates, capitalism tends towards the concentration of wealth and social inequality. A crucial point long made by the reproduction theorists is that the reproduction of class hierarchy depends not only on the transmission of different amounts of capital from parents to children but on different class-based social relationships—that is, differently distributed cultural and social capital.[38] In other words, the maintenance of the class hierarchy depends on the distribution of unequally valued knowledge, tastes, and dispositions and the means for acquiring them as well as the unequal distribution of social networks. The teaching of grit to the poor does not counter the reproduction of class hierarchy. It actually contributes to worsening it by teaching working class and poor children the dispositions, knowledge and tastes for subjugation in the public and private sectors. In other words, grit pedagogy is diametrically opposed to the dispositions towards dialogue, questioning, investigation, and dissent that are forms of cultural capital fostered in professional and ruling class schools charged with preparing future leaders across institutions of power. Grit repeats a tradition of teaching different senses of political and economic agency to different economic classes of students. Grit promotes a sense of agency for working class students defined by rule following and submission to authority rather than questioning authority and the relationship between knowledge and relations of power. The emphasis on submission to authority is ideal for preparing working class students for political marginalization rather than collective self-governance and for taking subordinate positions within the economy.

The narrative of trauma and alienation told in the biological discourse about grit presumes that healthy child development is a matter of successfully learning to internalize authority. It offers no sense of how, as both Erich Fromm's and Erik Erikson's critical human development theories suggest, healthy development involves ongoing crises of individuation—that is, the capacities for rationality, questioning, and autonomy crucially involve disobedience and refusal. Separation from symbolic authorities is necessary for development but the connection to community can be done in better or worse ways. Alienation in these theories is a prerequisite for reflectiveness about the self and the society. Yet, healthy adjustment involves expanding the capacities of the individual to comprehend and act on the alienating forces.[39] Grit mystifies the social sources of individual alienation by biologizing and naturalizing class inequality.

Grit and resilience frame individual and social problems in ways compatible with a politics of austerity that eviscerates the caregiving roles of the state. Grit as character education is inextricably linked to longer-standing academic expositions of student "resilience." Resilience studies in psychology and special education is a field that examines students in schools in poor communities where the majority of students succumb to the ill-effects of poverty, such as gang violence, imprisonment, and teenage pregnancy. Resilience studies does not ask how the social conditions of poverty and violence can be transformed or how students can learn to comprehend and act to change what oppresses them. Instead, resilience studies identifies the rare student who survives, graduates, and goes to university despite the social disinvestment, violence, targeting by the criminal justice system, despair, and poverty. Resilience studies focuses on the exceptional "success against all odds story." The thinking goes that if only the unique characteristics that allow for resilience can be identified, teachers, by replicating those unique characteristics, can design a course of action that might allow for more students to succeed in spite of the context. Grit shares with resilience studies a deeply conservative refusal to address radical disparities in social investment, the historical policy legacy that reproduces a racialized class hierarchy, the ways there are clear winners and losers, and the political pressure that maintains such radically unequal public spending patterns. Grit also shares with resilience studies the idealization of "getting out" of the context of poverty rather than learning to comprehend and confront the forces that produce it.

Grit as character education is also linked to a more recent claim on student agency in which knowledge and learning are radically estranged from the subjective experiences and contexts of the learners and from the objective social world. Grit is symbiotic with the above-mentioned banking education on steroids in the age of austerity, including the recent expansion of corporate–state coordinated standardized testing and standardization of curriculum and pedagogical approaches. Grit is diametrically opposed to a view of knowledge and learning in the tradition of critical pedagogy and progressive education, both of which treat knowledge as essential to comprehend individual experience, to reflect upon one's action, and to have such reflection become the basis for engaging with problems in the world. Rather, grit treats knowledge as akin to a commodity or money. Knowledge in this view is framed as being meaningful primarily as something that is consumed, regurgitated, and then exchanged—first for academic promotion but then for work, money, and consumption.

Grit can be seen as a kind of behavior code and pedagogical approach that corresponds to the dominant trends in neoliberal education reform. These reforms are grounded in a positivist denial of the framing values, assumptions, and ideologies behind the selection of truth claims and a denial of the values, assumptions, and ideologies involved in acts of interpretation. Grit, like reforms such as the standardized testing fetish, delinks knowledge from contexts, subjective experiences of students and teachers, and the broader social structures and formations that inform subjective experience.

Grit reinforces a description of educational processes that underlie consumer culture; that is, a feeling of scarcity in which the student is constantly denied the fulfillment of both desires and needs, through nobody's fault but her own. Both Tough and Duckworth are cognizant of the problem that if the end of self-denial is indulgence (in junk food, for example), then most people will take what they can get immediately rather than deferring gratification—especially people who are in a situation of greater stress and insecurity. Both discuss how candy tests of children's capacity for self-denial correlate to higher SAT scores, grades, and later income. Kids who can wait to eat one marshmallow or M&M in order to get a second one later have greater self-control. Duckworth laments that the seductions of consumption and advertising are greater than ever before and so demands on self-denial are greater than ever before.[40] Neither Duckworth nor Tough offer any way of thinking about the development of the subject in ways that criticize the ideology of consumerism or position its easy passivity and hyper-consumption as a form of human exploitation. Nor do they consider that different levels of hunger could possibly affect whether kids can control their consumption.[41]

The misleading suggestion is that individuals can employ grit to become whatever they desire (musician, Hollywood actor, politician, physicist). Proponents of "grit," then, avoid an honest admission about what grit is used to do in schools like KIPP: foster forms of learning defined by docility and submission to authority for the growing low-paid, low-skill bottom tier of the workforce. Grit does not foster dialogue, debate, investigation, and curiosity valued for leadership roles in the public and private sectors. Grit is misrepresented by proponents as opening a world of individual choices rather than discussed as a mode of educational and social control in the austere world of work defined by fewer and fewer choices as secure public sector work is scaled back, unemployment continuing at high levels. Thinking, questioning, and imagining are relentlessly assaulted in favor of the logic of accountability, standardization, and homogeneity enforced through corporeal control.[42]

What Tough and Duckworth and the other proponents of grit miss completely is that people are motivated by learning that is meaningful and relevant to their experiences and that such meaningful learning promises the power to comprehend and act on social realities. As both Paulo Freire and Henry Giroux have elaborated, learning that is meaningful and critical offers the potential for political agency rather than the consumer agency promised by grit. Unlike earlier conceptions of character education in which self-denial is yoked to the service of broader social, ethical, and political ends and visions, grit starts and ends with the lone individual as economic actor, worker, and consumer. If the end of self-denial is consumption, then why should anyone defer indulgence in short term pleasurable activities for learning that is only towards the end of yet more meaningless work for the end of consumption?

Grit celebrates and seeks to expand the death of the radical imagination—openness to imagining a future better than the present. Henry Giroux has insisted on the need for formative youth cultures in which radical imagination is fostered.[43] Paulo Freire put it concisely in suggesting that one must learn to denounce existing realities in order to announce an as yet unrealized future. Theory for all of these thinkers provides the means for youth to critically analyze the self and the society. Erich Fromm emphasized that such self- and social reflection as the means for social reconstruction begins not with obedience to authority (the core of grit) but rather disobedience.[44]

Erich Fromm's work provides a valuable diametrically opposed counterpoint to the recent popularization of grit. Fromm's developmental theory suggests that rationality depends upon disobedience to authority, that individual character must be understood as inseparable from social character, and that development involves constitutive crises that result from the disjuncture between the development of individual strengths and the process of individuation. Fromm's developmental theory highlights how individual development, that is, character formation, can only be understood in relation to social character. Individual experiences of alienation, estrangement, and isolation derive from the process of individuation, yet the social character informs how social relations are forged in ways that foster love and spontaneity, an embrace of others as human subjects rather than objects to possess, and a treatment of knowledge as dynamic. For Fromm, these developmental crises may be resolved badly in the form of the individual attempting to sadistically control, objectify, and inanimate objects, others, and knowledge, or masochistically abdicating freedom and agency to a magical helper, the all-powerful other. Or these crises of necessary individuation and alienation may be resolved well through learning to love and affirm spontaneous and free forms of life. While proponents of grit radically individualize alienation, Fromm sees individual alienation as inextricably informed by social forces. Freedom for grit is learned self-control harnessed to knowledge and activity that is beyond question. Freedom for Fromm as well as for Freire involves learning to question in order to learn to live spontaneously and creatively and to control with others those social phenomena that make people less free from domination.[45]

Fromm insists that the imposition of authority must be based in reason that is a universal and the acceptance of which does not constitute submission.[46] Rather domination comes from the imposition of irrational authority.[47] It is specifically the imposition of knowledge that is unexamined, the imposition of claims to truth that are beyond questioning that makes grit pedagogy authoritarian in its tendencies.

Austerity education is not only about a turn to repressive control of youth in the interest of amassing profits for the rich, creating a docile and disciplined workforce as the conditions of work and life are worsened for the majority of citizens. It is also about the right-wing project of capturing public space such as schools to actively produce politically illiterate, socially uncritical, and un-self-critical subject positions for youth to occupy. It involves a project of teaching teachers and students to understand learning and rationality as submission to authority, and miseducating them to comprehend their alienation as a failure of individual gumption rather than as a constitutive part of development informed by a social formation and economy that depends upon the making of alienation.

The turn to grit in educational reform comes at a moment of not only worsening pressures on labor, unprecedented inequalities in wealth and income, but also a growing misframed role for schools to end poverty and economic inequality which are driven principally by the class structure.[48] The most important role for public school is, rather, to foster the conditions for youth to imagine different futures of collective self-control that do not involve the pillage of nature and people.

Notes

1 David Harvey, *The Enigma of Capital* Oxford: Oxford University Press, 2010, 10–15.

2 Kenneth Saltman, *Capitalizing on Disaster: Taking and Breaking Public Schools* Boulder, CO: Paradigm Publishers, 2007; Henry Giroux, *On Critical Pedagogy* New York: Continuum, 2011; Michael Apple, *Educating the Right Way* New York: Routledge, 2005.

3 These privatizations are discussed in relation to both policy detail and critical pedagogical values in Henry Giroux, *Education and the Crisis of Public Values* New York: Peter Lang, 2010; and Kenneth Saltman, *The Failure of Corporate School Reform* Boulder, CO: Paradigm Publishers, 2012.

4 See Alexander Means, *Schooling in the Age of Austerity* New York: Palgrave Macmillan, 2013.

5 Recently these trends have been taken up differently by critical theorists and liberals. Critical theoretical discussion of these trends has been taken up in relation to broader questions of power, globalization, ideology, politics, cultural politics, and ethics and an assumption of the desirability of education

being implicated in fundamental social transformation by Kenneth Saltman, Henry Giroux, Kristen Buras, Michael Apple, David Hursh, Pauline Lipman, Lois Weiner, Alex Means, Clayton Pierce, Julia Hall, Mark Garrison among others. For liberal literature that largely affirms existing dominant social institutions and is reformist see, for example, Diane Ravitch, Linda Darling-Hammond, Richard Rothstein, Kevin Welner, Chris Lubienski.

6 See for example Henry Giroux, *Education and the Crisis of Public Values*; Michael Apple, *Educating the Right*.

7 Alexander Means, *Schooling in the Age of Austerity*; Kathleen Nolan, *Police in the Hallways: Discipline in an Urban High School* Minneapolis: University of Minnesota Press, 2011; Kenneth Saltman, and David Gabbard (eds.) *Education as Enforcement: the Militarization and Corporatization of Schools* 2nd edition New York: Routledge, 2010.

8 Sarah D. Sparks, "Nation's Report Card to Gather Data on Grit, Mindset" *Education Week* August 5, 2015, available at <www.edweek.org/ew/articles/2015/06/03/nations-report-card-to-gather-data-on.html>.

9 I take this up in detail in Kenneth Saltman, *The Gift of Education: Public Education and Venture Philanthropy* New York: Palgrave Macmillan, 2010.

10 For a recent brilliant treatment of this topic see Alexander Means, *Schooling in the Age of Austerity*.

11 See for example Kenneth Saltman, *Collateral Damage: Corporatizing Public Schools – a Threat to Democracy* Lanham, MD: Rowman & Littlefield, 2000; Saltman and Gabbard *Education as Enforcement*; Jeffrey Di Leo, Henry Giroux, Sophia McClennan and Kenneth Saltman, *Neoliberalism, Education, and Terrorism: Contemporary Dialogues* Boulder, CO: Paradigm Publishers, 2014; Henry Giroux, *Stealing Innocence: Corporate Culture's War on Youth* New York: Palgrave Macmillan, 2000; Chris Robbins, *Expelling Hope: The Assault on Youth and the Militarization of Schooling* Albany: SUNY Press, 2009.

12 Louis Althusser, "Ideology and Ideological State Apparatuses (Notes towards an Investigation)" in *Mapping Ideology* (edited) Slavoj Žižek New York: Verso, 1994, 100–40; Pierre Bourdieu and Jean-Claude Passeron, *Reproduction in Education, Society and Culture* 2nd edition Thousand Oaks, CA: Sage, 2000 (original 1977); Samuel Bowles and Herbert Gintis, *Schooling in Capitalist America* Chicago: Haymarket Books, 2011 (original 1976).

13 Giroux and Aronowitz rightly criticized the theoretical limitations of reproduction theory in groundbreaking books in the 1980s, such as Giroux, *Theory and Resistance in Education*; and Stanley Aronowitz and Henry Giroux, *Education Still Under Siege* Westport, CT: Bergin & Garvey, 1989. These limitations include its mechanistic tendencies, overemphasis on processes of domination at the expense of a focus on counter-hegemonic cultural production and resistance, and class-oriented if not economistic tendencies that make culture a reflection of economic structure.

14 Henry Giroux, *Youth in Revolt: Reclaiming a Democratic Future* Boulder, CO: Paradigm Publishers, 2013, 263.

15 Per pupil spending in Chicago public schools is about US$9000 while towns in the north shore suburbs spend about US$24,000. For a thorough report as to why equitable school funding matters see Bruce Baker, "Revisiting the Age-Old

Question: Does Money Matter in Education?" Albert Shanker Institute, 2012, available at <www.shankerinstitute.org/resource/does-money-matter>.

16 "Interview with Federal Reserve Chairman Ben Bernanke" *60 Minutes* December 5, 2010, available at < www.cbsnews.com/8301-504803_162-20024635-10391709.html>; Thomas L. Friedman, "The New Untouchables" *The New York Times* October 20, 2009, "Correspondent Steve Kroft Interviewed the President," 2010.

17 I take this up in detail in Kenneth Saltman, *The Failure of Corporate School Reform* Boulder, CO: Paradigm Publishers, 2012, 1–53.

18 In the US context Bowles and Gintis's *Schooling in Capitalist America* (1976) was the most significant early elaboration of reproduction theory. After being out of print for decades it has recently been re-released as: Samuel Bowles and Herbert Gintis, *Schooling in Capitalist America* Chicago: Haymarket Books, 2011.

19 For a brilliant discussion of the gendered dimensions of schooling in the service of the economy see Robin Truth Goodman, *Gender Work: Feminism After Neoliberalism.* New York: Palgrave Macmillan, 2013.

20 See Bowles and Gintis, *Schooling in Capitalist America.*

21 David Harvey, *The Enigma of Capital.*

22 Richard Wolff (film) *Capitalism Hits the Fan* (2009) Media Education Foundation.

23 William C. Symonds, "Education: A New Push to Privatize" *Business Week* January 13, 2002.

24 Nancy Fraser, "From Discipline to Flexibilization."

25 Koerth-Baker, "The Not-So-Hidden Cause behind the A.D.H.D. Epidemic."

26 Michel Foucault, *Discipline and Punish* New York: Vintage, 1977.

27 Bertell Ollman, "Why So Many Exams? A Marxist Response" *Z Magazine* October 2002.

28 My earliest two books *Collateral Damage* and *Education as Enforcement* both developed this concept of "education as enforcement" as a distinct transformation in the neoliberalization of public education.

29 The language of "grit" invokes nineteenth century American exceptionalism, westward expansion, and a romanticization of a brutal survivalism traded on in recent films such as the Coens' *True Grit* and NBC TV's use of the same title in covering grit as character education Rock Center [NBC TV Program] "True Grit: Teaching Character Skills in the Classroom" September 27, 2012.

30 Paul Tough, *How Children Succeed: Grit, Curiosity, and the Hidden Power of Character* New York: Houghton Mifflin Harcourt, 2012, 136.

31 The "grit scale" was developed by the lead academic empirical researcher of grit Angela Duckworth and can be accessed at <www.sas.upenn.edu/~duckwort/images/12-item%20Grit%20Scale.05312011.pdf>.

32 See, for example, the website of the program Tools of the Mind available at <www.toolsofthemind.org/philosophy/self-regulation/>.

33 Paulo Freire, *Pedagogy of the Oppressed* New York: Continuum, 1972.

34 The empty vessel version of education begins with Locke and Rousseau while the fullest exposition of learned self-regulation can be found in Kant and was criticized by Michel Foucault.

35 See for example, Immanuel Kant's "Lectures on Pedagogy" *Philosophy of Education: The Essential Texts* (edited) Steven M. Cahn New York: Routledge, 2009, 253–80. For the elaboration of learned self-discipline towards moral ends and Immanuel Kant, "Answer to the Question: What is Enlightenment?" in *Basic Writings of Kant* (edited) Allen W. Wood New York: Modern Library, 2001, 133–42 on education for the public use of reason.

36 See Aristotle, "Nicomachean Ethics" *Philosophy of Education: The Essential Texts* (edited) Steven M. Cahn New York: Routledge, 2009, 109–32.

37 Tough, *How Children Succeed*, xx.

38 Bourdieu and Passeron, *Reproduction in Education*.

39 See Erich Fromm, *Escape from Freedom* New York: Henry Holt, 1994 (original 1941) and Erik Erikson, *Identity: Youth, and Crisis* New York: W.W. Norton, 1994 (originally 1968).

40 See Angela Duckworth (lecture) "Will Power, Grit, Self-Control, and Achievement" Family Action Network November 29, 2012, available online at <www.youtube.com/watch?v=7ALmzoWRQMo>.

41 Robin Truth Goodman personal communication.

42 See Henry Giroux's recent articles on the assault on critical pedagogy, political literacy, and thinking itself in both education and popular culture on truthout. org.

43 See for example Henry Giroux, "The Disimagination Machine and the Pathologies of Power" *symplokē* 21(1–2) (2013), 257–69.

44 See Erich Fromm, *On Disobedience: Why Freedom Means Saying "No" to Power* New York: Harper Perennial Modern Thought, 2010 (original 1981).

45 See Fromm, *Escape from Freedom* and Paulo Freire, *Pedagogy of the Oppressed*, who relies on and develops Fromm's theory of subject formation.

46 See Fromm, *On Disobedience*. A similar position can be found in Noam Chomsky, *Chomsky on Democracy and Education* (edited by C.P. Otero) New York: Routledge, 2002, and Noam Chomsky and Donaldo Macedo, *Chomsky on Miseducation* Lanham, MD: Rowman & Littlefield, 2004.

47 Fromm, *On Disobedience*, 8.

48 Bowles and Gintis, *Schooling in Capitalist America*, 49.

3

BIOMETRIC ANALYTIC PEDAGOGY

Control of Students and Teachers, and the Assault on Thinking

Introduction: Biometric Control

In the summer of 2012, news reports revealed that the Bill and Melinda Gates Foundation had funded research on the biometric measurement of student bodies. The US$1.4 million research involved collecting students' physical reactions to teachers' lessons by having students wear biometric bracelets (Q Sensors) that run an electric current across the skin to measure changes in electrical charges "as the sympathetic nervous system responds to stimuli."[1] "The sensors detect excitement, stress, fear, engagement, boredom, and relaxation through the skin."[2]

While the electrodes are applied to the bodies of the students, it is the behavior of the teachers that is primarily being measured: teaching practice is supposedly manifest on the bodies of children. In fact, the Q Sensor research shares the Gates' passion for data mining and for standardizing both teaching practice and school models towards the end of creating the fewest efficient delivery systems or methodologies.[3] A prior Gates project measured the teachers' effect on students by videotaping 20,000 classroom lessons and analyzing teacher behavior minute to minute and second to second in search of how teachers' behaviors corresponded to students' standardized test scores. These corporeal measurement projects also involve prior Gates survey research of 100,000 children about teacher behavior and, likewise, efforts to discern relationships between common teacher practice and standardized test outcomes.

Two biometric companies Affectiva and SensorStar Labs have developed another biometric tool that is being tested on students and teachers.

Facial recognition algorithms measure the students' facial expressions with webcams, analyze facial movement, and generate feedback reports to teachers. This technology interprets the meaning of a smile or frown, scrunched or widened eyes, the changed distance between the corner of the mouth and the corner of the eye. The facial movement is then categorized based in comparisons of facial movements with thousands of subjects' feelings. Affectiva's Affdex facial recognition program claims to measure "valence"—positive or negative experience of the image or object as measured by smiles relative to frown, scowls, and nose wrinkles. "Attention" measures are determined by whether the subject is looking directly at the screen or is distracted and physically turned away. "Expressiveness" measures purport to determine emotional engagement with the object regardless of positive or negative valence by calculating the frequency and intensity of positively and negatively associated facial expressions.[4] The primary use of facial emotional measurement technology has been to develop emotionally potent and engaging advertisements by gauging the viewers' physical response to ads. However, predominant consumer marketing applications have been expanding to include voter marketing and classroom teaching.

Not surprisingly, a number of teachers and scholars have responded to the biometric educational measurement projects by describing them as "Orwellian."[5] The invocation of Orwell rightly suggests that biometric measurements of student attention are an expression of intrusive, overbearing, and totalitarian government treatment of individuals. Yet the invocation of Orwell also suggests that these projects are unusual, exceptional, and an aberration to a system that does not otherwise share its animating values. Henry Giroux has been one of the few voices to valuably situate these projects in relation to the rising security state and broader political movement towards totalitarianism.[6]

My contention in this chapter is that biometric measurement for pedagogy may appear unusual or extreme in terms of the broader field of education but that the underlying assumptions and logic animating the practice are thoroughly consistent with the dominant values and ideologies about teaching, learning, and knowledge animating dominant educational reform trends. Most centrally, these biometric education projects share with such dominant reforms as Common Core State Standards, Every Student Succeeds Act, edTPA, and CAEP assumptions that:

1. Knowledge ought to be comprehended as akin to a deliverable commodity. Moreover, the delivery of such knowledge can be controlled

for efficiency, and knowledge as a deliverable thing is politically neutral and universally valuable.

2. Knowledge does not need to be comprehended in relation to broader objective realities and social struggles—that is, in relation to the social totality.

3. Knowledge does not need to be comprehended in relation to subjective experience and individual and group difference.

4. If interpretation and judgment are to have any place in pedagogy, then it is towards the end of problem solving skills not towards the end of comprehending the social and individual meaning of knowledge.

What is worrying about biometric education projects is not only that they represent a form of learning defined by control over the body and behavior of teachers and students but also that they represent an effort to eradicate forms of pedagogy in which questioning, thinking, interpretation, and judgment are central and in which the inevitable cultural politics of knowledge are denied through recourse to biology. Understood in this way, biometric analytics as the basis for pedagogy puts in place practices that actively produce students as passive consumer subjects and teachers as deskilled delivery technicians responsible for delivering knowledge of someone else's making. Biometric analytic pedagogy proposes a relationship between a student and teacher that is based on the relationship between a screen viewer and a media product rather than one between a teacher and a student.

It is crucial to make an initial distinction between the most common use of biometric technology in schools for surveillance and identification and what I am examining here—namely, biometric learning technology and teacher assessment projects. Biometric measurement devices are mostly being expanded in schools for the identification of students and teachers. For example, fingerprint, iris scan, or facial recognition programs are being used to ascertain student attendance, verification of students in taking tests in school or at home online.[7] Biometric technology is being debated for use in teacher access to gun lockers and is interwoven with security and even the militarization or prisonization of schools. These identification programs are designed for surveillance, monitoring, and control.[8] My concern here, however, is specifically with the use of biometric analytic technology in pedagogy that is designed to measure teacher efficacy through the bodies of youth.

In the sections that follow I first explain biometric pedagogy as a new form of Taylorism that furthers and reworks the earliest theories and ideologies of business efficiencies but with the student as the object of work. Then I examine how such biometric education projects as the Q Sensor bracelet and Facial Affect programs share a set of assumptions about education:

1. that learning should be stimulating and entertaining like television;
2. that learning is passive;
3. that good teaching captures student attention rather than engaging in dialogic exchange or dispositions for questioning, investigation, and experimentation;
4. that knowledge can be delivered;
5. that delivery of knowledge can be measured by both physical measures of receptivity and by standardized tests;
6. that standardized test scores can be increased by forcing teachers to do more efficient teaching behaviors as measured by student bodies, and that the cause of a "deficit" of student learning can be understood as a lack of disciplined teacher behavior.

The biometrics project furthers the longstanding Gates Foundation assumption that educational improvement ought to focus centrally on changing teacher behavior rather than on addressing how the social context for education affects learning. Reducing education to teacher behavior ignores the impacts of both poverty and the unequal distribution of cultural capital—that is, differently distributed socially valued knowledge, taste, and dispositions and the means to acquire them.[9] Put differently, Gates' pedagogy disregards how the economic and symbolic hierarchies informing the treatment of students' bodies and minds in schools result in radically different treatment and outcomes.

In a manner reminiscent of *A Clockwork Orange,* the Gates Foundation sees motivation as an issue that has less to do with students' values, passions, and curiosity than with physical stimulation. Speaking on behalf of the Gates Foundation, Deborah Robinson defended the Q Sensor project explaining that in the past biometric technology had been used with autistic children "to show those who might seem unresponsive to external stimuli are engaged and learning."[10] The biometric research, however, does not aim to overcome a defect in affect on the part of students that would limit a teacher's capacity to gauge interest. Instead, the technology is meant to ignore the values, interests, and ideals of teachers, and also ignore that which might be meaningful to students as the basis for individual and social agency. Biometric educational technology appeals to the way that classroom stimulus works most directly on the body.

The Gates' obsession with translating teaching into metrics and numerically quantifiable outcomes has an historical antecedent in behaviorism, Taylorism, and scientific management approaches to industrial worker efficiency that were widely touted for educational reform since the early twentieth century. It is also similar to the more contemporary efforts of industrial psychologists and marketing experts to measure children's reactions to marketing campaigns designed to target parents with the "nag factor."[11] It also shares a likeness with audience rating tests for films and TV shows.

The rise of biometric measurement has to be understood as part of a structural remaking of public education through privatization in which under the guise of consumer choice, technology products promoted by massive media education corporations are in fact replacing teacher and community control over educational practice, pedagogy, and curriculum. This structural change is being promoted economically by the development of adaptive learning technologies and online curriculum and data management products that, as I discuss in the next chapter, displace the work of teachers and administrators with corporations. The structural change is also being promoted politically by right-wing think tanks that seek to "de-bundle" the public school. That is, the rightist project is promoted under the guise of technological progress to sell off and contract out every imaginable function of the public school.[12]

The New New Taylorism:[13] Controlling the Body

In the last fifteen years, critical education scholars have pointed out how the rise of high stakes standardized testing represents a new Taylorism in education. Taylorism, or scientific management, was launched at the start of the twentieth century by Frederick Taylor, who sought to introduce a "science" of business management. His primary aim was to create labor efficiencies by eradicating waste in the labor process. Taylor saw management's role in production as developing and actively implementing scientific programs of time and movement efficiency. Taylorism calls for breaking down the work process into the fewest possible subtasks to decrease the time, movement, and energy used by the worker. Taylor preached the universal virtue of efficiencies created by disciplining workers to carry more pig iron or lay more bricks in a day—right up to the point of physical failure. While the owner of the industry benefitted from producing more in the same time, Taylor falsely believed that this meant that the worker earned more in the same time. In fact, the work speed ups that Taylor promoted allowed more work to be extracted from a given worker for the same labor cost while creating greater competition among workers and driving wages down.

Taylor believed that workers were mentally incapable of knowing how to manage themselves through the "scientific" approach. Workers should be treated as dumb animals or machines. Taylor's scientific management formed the basis of modern business education. It also, more pertinent to our purposes, was imported into education in the early twentieth century by Franklin Bobbitt and others applying a factory production model to schooling.[14] Taylorism modeled the time and space of school on the factory, and treated knowledge and curriculum as the domain of specialized expert managers and teachers as delivery agents aiming for efficiency, framing students as the "raw materials" of the production process.[15] In short, as critical education scholars in the 1970s and 1980s pointed out, Taylorism participated in instituting a hidden curriculum of capitalism within a public system. As E. Wayne Ross contends, while the modern workplace has moved on to flexible specialization and lean production, not to mention a service-based rather than industrial factory economy, the US school is still rooted firmly in the factory model.[16]

Critical education scholars in the 1970s and 1980s took aim at the legacy of Taylorism or scientific management as part of a broader left criticism of the ways that public schooling was implicated in reproducing class and cultural hierarchy, and undermining the development of politically engaged forms of civic education. In this discourse, critical scholars such as Henry Giroux and Stanley Aronowitz highlighted how scientific management as a cult of efficiency was also involved in actively denying the politics of schooling and curriculum.[17] Today, this insight could not be more relevant as biometric education and other approaches to controlling student and teacher bodies impose a political agenda for schooling under the guise of disinterested objectivity and neutrality.

Following the early 2000s launch of No Child Left Behind and its instituting of high stakes standardized testing, a number of critics have described the testing regime as a "new Taylorism" that, as Wayne Au puts it, "is promoting the standardization of teaching that both disempowers and deskills teachers"(Au, 2011: 30). High stakes testing intensifies an efficacy model of teaching in which numerically quantified outputs must be sought by teachers and administrators. With federal funds contingent upon increased test scores, such standardization results in teaching to the tests, gutting out courses and programs of study that are not tested such as arts, music, and physical education. The standardization trend also mutilates the study of language, literature, and history into skills-based curricula. Worse yet are the federally mandated forms of deskilling that have been radically expanded, such as scripted "teacher-proof" lessons in which the last shred of teacher autonomy, reflection, and participation in curriculum and pedagogy planning is removed from the teaching process (Au, 2011: 32).

Biometric education not only reduces knowledge to that which is numerically quantifiable, standardizes teaching practice, and decreases teacher autonomy like the standardized testing trend but it also physically measures students' biological reactions to teaching. In a sense, biometric education is a return to a more direct form of Taylorism, in which the labor of the worker, the teacher, is subject to physical measurement. Yet, there is a twist. In Frederick Taylor's studies of the ironworker moving pieces of pig iron and the bricklayer laying bricks, the body of the worker is measured by quantifying the object of labor. With biometrics the labor of the teacher is measured by the "thing" moved, the body of a child. The child is the thing measured to influence and control the labor of the worker towards greater alleged efficiencies. In this schema, if the child is assumed to be a physical object to be moved, then the teacher is assumed to be a thoughtless performer of a prescribed series of behaviors. Thinking resides elsewhere.

The Gates' education agenda and its efforts to revive Taylorism in public schooling share a longstanding assumption that is diametrically opposed to the traditions of progressive and critical education. The progressive and critical educational traditions presume that knowledge ought to be meaningful, relevant, and interesting to students so that teachers can problematize knowledge in relation to broader social forces that produce that knowledge and experience. In the progressive and critical traditions, students learn how what they experience is in part produced by broader social institutions, forces, and systems such that they can comprehend and challenge what they experience as oppressive. In this view, knowledge, which is created through unequal dialogic exchange, forms the basis for identifying and denaturalizing oppression and domination as well as the basis for agency—the capacity to act on and shape the social world. Claims to truth in school can be made meaningful by investigating them in relation to the individual problems that students experience. Critical pedagogies can further what C. Wright Mills described as the aim of critical sociology, to translate individual problems into public problems.

Seven Assumptions in Biometric Pedagogy

Assumption 1: Learning should be stimulating and entertaining like television

Contrary to critical forms of education, the Gates' projects aim to enforce the acquisition of official knowledge, whether or not it is decontextualized, meaningless, and boring. By appealing directly to the body and its physical stimulation, biometric education seeks to replace teacher aspirations to expand student curiosity with the kind of physiological excitation characteristic of television spectatorship and, more specifically, with the visceral excitation stimulated by advertising. The crucial concern of advertising is to stimulate viewers to forge lasting positive brand impressions and to associate a product with a broader dreamworld of consumption. Moreover, the biometric focus on the body as locus of learning rejects the critical pedagogical tradition that aims to develop in students the active capacity for critical consciousness. That is, in the critical pedagogical tradition, knowledge is estranged, denaturalized, and objectified in order to consider it in terms of its conditions of production, including the material and symbolic interests animating claims to truth. Knowledge is seen as being produced through always unequal dialogic exchange.

On the contrary, classroom teaching in the biometric view is a one way street. It is imagined as an entertaining or boring TV show or advertisement traveling from the screen (the teacher) to the viewer (the student) rather than as part of a dialogue and exchange with students. It positions students as passive consumers of static knowledge rather than as participants in active inquiry and knowledge making. As the makers of Affectiva's facial recognition products contend, the value of Affdex is that it reveals what students find stimulating. The all too obvious question is why not *ask* the students what is stimulating, interesting, or uninteresting? And, why? Such dialogue potentially opens into a discussion about the subjective experience of the student, how the student is interpreting, articulating, and thinking about this experience, and the ways that that subjective experience is formed by forces in the objective world. Biometric measurement of stimulation, attention, and valence presumes to bypass dialogue and thought. Biometric education thus corresponds closely with the anti-dialogic positioning of standardized testing as the final arbiter of learning. Those who made the tests are not in a dialogue with those who take them. Hence, they cannot be questioned as to their evidence, motives, and values. But biometric education goes a step further to presume that the truth of interest and motivation can be read off of the body itself. Biometric educational projects and products display a deep distrust of thought, questioning, consciousness, and mediation.

Assumption 2: Learning is passive

By appealing to physiological stimulation, biometric educational pedagogies are modeled on consumerist modes of passive reception. Such "edutainment" presumes that greater learning derives from greater entertainment, stimulation, and pleasure as measured by certain physical stimulation. Such an equation of learning with passive reception disregards modes of learning in which the learner actively pursues, questions, doubts, and disagrees. Moreover, the passive conception of learning is at odds with dialogic learning as conceived through active discussion, exchange, dynamism, and spontaneity. Consider different ways of watching an advertisement or television show. While biometric analytics presumes to measure a student passively watching a teacher perform, this is modeled on a TV watcher passively watching a show. Passive reception of media differs from, for example, viewing practices informed by critical media literacy. Critical media literacy teaches the viewer to analyze and criticize the narrative, the ideologies, and how the representation relates to broader political, economic, and cultural forces, struggles, and discourses as well as what kinds of subject positions and forms of identification are produced by the representation.[18] Biometric analytics does not aim to measure the extent to which students are stimulated to question what they see and engage in dialogue with the teacher about it. Nor does it aim to measure the quality or intensity of dialogic exchange. Instead, it aims to measure the teacher as a screen that the student watches. In this case, not dialogic learning but monologic learning is presumed to be of value.

Biometric analytic pedagogy puts forward a particular political perspective on pedagogy that Paulo Freire described as "banking education" and that philosophically can be traced back to early empiricists such as John Locke who presumed the child to be a blank slate or an empty vessel to be filled with knowledge. Part of the allure of biometric analytic pedagogy is its appeal to nature and apparently disinterested, neutral, and objective science—that is, its positivist ideology. After all, as it is the body that is being measured for its physical changes caused by teacher actions, then the truth of the teacher behavior can be transparently read in the bio-measurements. In other words, the turn to the body, its stimulation and disposition as the measure of the value of teaching, conceals the most crucial questions that have to do with the relationships between cognition, consciousness, and pedagogy: What is it in this knowledge that students find meaningful? Why do they find it meaningful? How is it meaningful in relation to their lived experience? Whose values, perspectives, ideas, interests and ideologies are represented by this knowledge? What forces in the world are at play in producing this knowledge? And, how does comprehending the forces and struggles at play in producing knowledge transform what the individual can do with the knowledge socially and politically?

Assumption 3: Good teaching captures student attention rather than engaging in dialogic exchange or dispositions for questioning, investigation, and experimentation

Biometric analytic pedagogy presumes that good teaching captures attention the way that advertising competes for scarce attention on a web browser or TV commercials compete for attention against bathroom breaks or other channels that can be surfed. While the commercial project of capturing attention has exploded, it is both relatively recent historically and highly contradictory. As Jonathan Crary points out, the claim of an epidemic of "attention deficit" that is most frequently blamed on screens makes no sense in a society and economy predicated on distractions.[19] Attention is something that only begins as a concept in the nineteenth century, and there have been theories of attention that celebrate the possibilities of focused attention (William James)[20] but also its opposite, distraction (Walter Benjamin).[21] This contradiction continues today as youth are medicated at epidemic proportions for attention deficit disorder and ADHD and prescribed amphetamines to pay attention to that which might otherwise be uninteresting, meaningless, or drudgery. The American Academy of Pediatricians partly blames an excess of screen time in early childhood for the epidemic. Yet, the opposite is also the case as elderly people with difficulties paying attention are encouraged by the health and medical industries to expand their attention capacities by playing video games.[22] In other words, the poison for youth is being prescribed as the medicine for the old. The capacity for multi-tasking, which is in fact the fast switching of attention, appears elastic. The key point here is that attention has been made into a problem for youth specifically with regard to a form of schooling in which decontextualized knowledge in the form of heavy standardized testing and canned curriculum has become dominant.

Biometric analytic pedagogy measures the teacher's performance at capturing and keeping youth attention in a broader media-saturated context in which incessant, fast cut screen-based stimulation is the norm. The model of teachers performing as if on a TV screen assures that the teaching will not engage with students and their experiences, or seek to comprehend what makes knowledge meaningful to students. But the measure of attention is the wrong measure anyway. This issue of capturing and measuring attention is inextricably related to the question of what is meaningful and motivating to students. Biometric analytic pedagogy's emphasis on attention capture presumes a conception of motivation for attention that is infantile at best. It is akin to a set of jangled keys in front of an infant. Yet, as the infant develops, she develops interests beyond shiny objects. These motivating interests at an early age involve abstract concepts and questions as to unseen causes. Three- and four-year-old children get interested, for example, in space flight, floating in places with less gravity, why it rains, how come some people do not have homes, and why and how these things are possible. Screens are highly effective at habituating children and adults to repose in a disposition for passive stimulated receptivity. Biometric pedagogy encourages people to accept passive stimulated receptivity as an ideal pedagogical situation because of the possibility for it to be measurable. The preferable pedagogical situation is one of dialogue, and dialogue is far less measurable. In other words, biometric pedagogy is at odds with the dialogue one does with oneself that involves asking why or "talking back" to a person or a text. Disobedience to the authority of the teacher or text that is possible in dialogue is factored out of the mode of learning in passive reception. In this sense, passive reception is akin to the affirmation of dogma.

One scholar who has become widely read, cited, and influential on technological attention capture in the humanities, Bernard Stiegler, rightly worries about the overuse of screen technology by youth but misses the important relationship between thinking and disobedience. In *Taking Care of Youth and the Generations*, Stiegler contends that the danger of heavy screen use by children is that it undermines attention by disrupting the child's primary identification with the parent.[23] He claims that education is for transmitting social competency that produces responsibility. The problem is that Stiegler wrongly defines education through transmission and reception of generational authority rather than seeing education for the possibilities of dialogic exchange and autonomy. For Stiegler, media destroys attention by destroying the psyche's resistance to the pleasure principle and attention in the child can only be formed through an intergenerational relationship. It seems to make more sense to comprehend attention as coming out of experience that is meaningful: What becomes meaningful and of interest to a person? The tradition of critical pedagogy suggests that what one experiences can be problematized and theorized in terms of the conditions of the making of the experience. As Henry Giroux writes,

> a critical approach to education illuminates the relationships among knowledge, authority, and power. Critical forms of pedagogy raise questions regarding who has control over the conditions for the production of knowledge. Is the production of knowledge and curricula in the hands of teachers, textbook companies, corporate interests, the elite or other forces? Central to the perspective informing critical pedagogy is the recognition that education is always implicated in power relations because it offers particular version and visions of civic life, community, the future, and how we might construct representations of ourselves, others, and our physical and social environment.[24]

What becomes meaningful and of interest is both the reconstructed experience, the original experience, and the sense of power in comprehending how the theorized experience and newly perceived reality can become the basis for social analysis and action. This way of comprehending attention is radically at odds with Stiegler's in that while Stiegler links learning to the inheritance of knowledge and the internalization of parental value and authority, critical pedagogy links learning to acts of interpretation that can form the basis for social agency. Stiegler, while a critic of the dangers of corporate media production and influence on youth, has a deeply conservative sense of learning and agency that fails to comprehend what Fromm (who influenced Freire), Erikson, and other critical developmental psychologists have suggested about the development of identity. These developmental psychologists have shown healthy ego development, consciousness, and the growth of intelligence as demanding necessary individuation from parental authority. As Fromm insists, rationality and the possibility of dialogue itself begins with disobedience. Responsibility begins not with total identification but rather with disidentification, with a break from obedience, with the alienating act of questioning.

Assumption 4: Knowledge can be "delivered"

What pedagogy should be aiming for is to be meaningful to students. However, being meaningful is not enough. Critical pedagogy emphasizes that learning should be meaningful in order to begin a process of self and social analysis that can result in learning being the basis for social power. To be meaningful, pedagogy must relate knowledge to what students know from experience and also relate it to broader social realities informing their experience. Meaningful pedagogy can be problematized and be made socially critical to form the basis for students to have a sense of political agency, to be able to comprehend their experiences, and to comprehend the social world such that they can act on and shape the social world. Biometric analytic pedagogy presumes that if teachers can stimulate youth, then the students will become receptive to whatever the teacher is teaching (selling). As such, biometric analytic pedagogy is modeled on consumer agency rather than political agency. Consumer agency works with advertising to emotionally associate a brand or product with a fantasy of consumption and ultimately the act of buying. Biometric analytic pedagogy positions youth as consumer agents to consume knowledge and ultimately regurgitate it back on standardized tests. The point here is not that biometric pedagogy cannot be meaningful but that the meanings are limited to that which is stimulating and titillating in the immediacy. To make meaningful learning critical and transformative may require the student to feel discomfort with existing reality. Existing unfreedom must be denounced so that students imagine a different future. Biometric pedagogy remains trapped in the positive—in affirmation of what is.

Assumption 5: Delivery of knowledge can be measured by the body and by standardized tests to maximize efficiencies of knowledge delivery

A crucial assumption of biometric analytic pedagogy is that the truth of learning can be discerned directly from the body itself. Physiological stimulation is presumed to signal receptivity of knowledge. Of course, this raises the question of what if what is being taught is false but stimulating. For example, biometric analytics might be useful for in some ways measuring receptivity to propaganda (which is what advertising used to be called), but how can it measure the way that students mediate what they receive? One would hope, for example, that good schooling would provide the tools to analyze and criticize not just propaganda but the ways that knowledge and truth-claims are related to particular group interests and perspectives—that is, the political nature of knowledge. Biometric analytic pedagogy has no way of dealing with the ways students interpret, resist, selectively appropriate, judge, and mull what they learn nor how such interpretation and mediation is informed by the broader social forces that form subjectivity.

If learning can be read off of the body as a biological effect, then not only is learning conceived wrongly as a deposit of knowledge into an empty vessel but there is no role for the distinctly human uses of language and culture. The-biometric-analytic-pedagogical presumption of "learning" shares similarities with the discredited theory of behaviorism and its assumption that learning is best understood as physical conditioning. In fact, as a theory of learning, biometric pedagogy offers even less than behaviorism. Behaviorism assumes that teachers' actions can, through positive or negative reinforcement, determine student behavior. Biometric analytic pedagogy measures not behavior but the physiological effect of the teacher's behavior on the body of the student. It does not matter what the student thinks, nor what the student does or how they act. What matters is what the body does. There is a preposterous assumption that truth about learning resides in the body and, moreover, that this measurement of it is more "objective" than the subjective language, interpretation, culture, and mediation ignored by such measurement of learning. The deception here is parallel to the deceptive concealment of subjectivity that happens with other positivist pedagogical forms such as standardized testing. The test makers' subjective perspectives and social positions are concealed in the formation of questions and possible right answers. The test taker's subjectivity and social position likewise is disregarded as an obstacle to the allegedly universally valuable truth of the test questions. As well, the teacher's subjectivity and social position are disregarded as irrelevant to the practice of teaching. If teaching becomes reading a script or adhering to prescribed behavioral recipes, then, indeed, the subjectivity of the teacher may not matter to what is being "taught." However, this teacher behavior cannot be regarded as teaching in any meaningful sense in that the teacher becomes interchangeable with an inert object such as a script or a machine. What is gutted out of the teaching process in this case is spontaneity, dynamism, exchange, and the possibility of learning through investigation, curiosity, and asking why. Beyond this, what is gutted out of the teaching process is the possibility of praxis in Freire's sense—the possibility of reflective action in which the world and the experience of it become the object of knowledge. In this view, learning aims to reconstruct the meaning of the world and experience in order to act on and shape collectively the world that one inhabits towards the vocation of humanization. Humanization in this view means being a subject with the power to act on the social world rather than being an object acted on by others.

Assumption 6: Standardized test scores can be increased by forcing teachers to perform more efficient teaching behaviors as measured by student bodies

The biometric analytic measurement projects presume that effective and efficient teaching can be objectively measured by standardized tests. As already discussed, there is a mistaken assumption that student learning can be read off of the body as if the student were an object and that the quality of the teaching is linked to the performance or enforcement of the right pedagogical behaviors. These false assumptions which presume a positivist conception of learning are linked in biometric analytic pedagogy following the mistaken view that standardized testing can be an objective and disinterested measure of learning. Standardized tests conceal the animating values, interests, and ideologies behind the selection of knowledge, the framing of questions, and the proposed answers. That is, standardized tests remove the subjectivity and social position of the test maker from the matter of what knowledge is claimed as valuable and beyond question and interpretation. This radically empiricist approach treats knowledge as a collection of facts that appear to come from nowhere and no one. Biometric analytic pedagogy stitches together three positivist moves that disregard the relationship between subjectivity and learning, and that disregard the relationship between learning and the ways knowledge and subjectivity are produced by objective social forces and realities. Move one is the treatment of the body of the learner as the arbiter of the truth of learning. Move two is the treatment of the body of the teacher as a kind of machine that needs to perform in a singular efficient fashion. Move three is the treatment of knowledge as standardizable and testable. Biometric analytic pedagogy puts these three moves together as an allegedly objective and neutral system of measuring learning. Yet, what is actively denied in this approach is the class and cultural differences of different students and teachers.

Assumption 7: The cause of a "deficit" of student learning can be understood as a lack of disciplined teacher behavior

By falsely grounding the truth of knowledge in positivist standardized tests and falsely grounding the truth of learning in the biology of the student, biometric analytic pedagogy sets the stage for claiming that teacher behavior is the variable element that needs to be controlled. Knowledge and the student are falsely positioned as constants. Thus the teacher's behavior can be prescribed and the allegedly most efficient methodologies can be enforced on the teacher, applied universally.

In the last few years there has been a frenzied push coming in part from the Bill and Melinda Gates Foundation and right-wing think tanks to claim that the quality of the teacher is the only element or the decisive element that matters for good schooling. This position not only wrongly equates learning with standardized test scores it problematically suggests that the changes in test scores can be understood as the effect of "good" teaching rather than replacement of teaching with mindless test-prep drills. The social use of the claim is to disregard all of the other requirements that go into the full support of schools including the physical site, competent administration, the amount of prep time and material support supplied to teachers, the economic and social conditions of students and so on. Moreover, this myopic view of teaching disregards the role that class and cultural symbolic hierarchies play in the cultural capital that students bring into schools and that schools reward or punish.

Putting the onus for the performance of the school and the civil society exclusively on the teacher allows for all of these factors to be disregarded which assures that redistributive efforts and critical educational projects to improve public schools can be avoided by those who stand to benefit from the current grossly unjust arrangement.

Conclusion: Biometric Pedagogy Sets the Stage for Use of Data

Biometric analytic pedagogy has to be seen as necessarily tied to the growing trend to capture and parse "big data" about students. Big data involves the collection of data from multiple media sources and the use of analytic models to draw correlations between seemingly disparate information. Venture philanthropists such as the Eli and Edythe Broad Foundation and the Bill and Melinda Gates Foundation have been promoting the expanded use of student data, to inform teaching practice and educational administration, while the federal Race to the Top program incentivized states to expand data collection projects. Some of these projects are supposed to track student test scores over time and contribute to projects such as value added modeling that aims to replace unionized secure teacher work with teacher work that is evaluated in terms of raised test scores. Broad, for example, also promotes forms of educational leadership that are "data driven." Other uses of data now include the development of adaptive learning systems in which the data from participants is used to modify the computer-based lesson and the data generated by the student participating is used to formulate future lessons and expectations from the student. As well, as the next chapter details, large media corporations such as News Corp are selling hardware and standardized curriculum software. The rise of biometric analytic pedagogy has to be seen as one means by which, increasingly, corporations and states are capturing data about students and then putting this data through algorithmic predictive models. The significance of these predictive models cannot be overestimated in terms of how data is becoming the basis to track, sort, and sift students in order to reproduce historical inequalities under the guise of disinterested "science." As well, these data manipulations are required by federal and state reporting laws that local districts cannot accommodate. As a consequence, for profit companies are playing an expanding role in accumulating student data, analyzing it, and selling it.

There are vast privacy questions with this new use of student data as seen, for example, in the parental backlash against InBloom—the database student tracking project that was promoted and implemented by venture philanthropists. Yet, despite widespread concerns, there is little that regulates how data such as that collected by biometric analytic pedagogy will be used, entered into automated learning systems, and form the basis for presumed and pre-programmed directives for different groups of students. Moreover, the use of such data as a basis for prescribing teacher behavior and evaluating teacher performance is uncharted territory. Perhaps the greatest dangers, aside from the turn against thinking and dialogic forms of pedagogy and the turn to corporeal control, is the concealment of the values implicit in such projects and the mistaken allure of "disinterested science" through recourse to numbers derived from measuring the body. In this sense wariness of biometric pedagogy ought to be considered in relation to the rapid rise of automated learning systems (discussed in the next chapter) that, like biometric pedagogy, sort and sift students by concealing the politics of knowledge and culture. The serious questioning of biometric analytic pedagogy has to be linked to a revived refusal of the positivist ideology that has driven the standardized testing and standardization of curriculum movements and that has deeply anti-intellectual tendencies. As well, the development of biometric pedagogy needs to be situated in terms of the broader expansion of material and symbolic hierarchical, anti-democratic, and inegalitarian social relations that have deepened in the economy, the political system, and the culture.

Notes

1 Glenda Kwek, "Brains and Bracelets: Gates Funds Wrist Sensors for Students" *The Sydney Morning Herald* June14, 2012, available at <www.smh.com.au>.
2 Kwek, ibid.
3 I take up the Gates Foundation reduction of teaching quality to individual teacher behavior and the efforts to "replicate" and "scale up" school models at length in Saltman, *The Gift of Education*.
4 See "White Paper Exploring the Emotion Classifiers behind Affdex Facial Coding," 3. Available at <www.affdex.com/clients/affdex-resources/>.
5 Henry A. Giroux, "When Schools Become Dead Zones of the Imagination" August 13, 2013 Truthout.org, available at <www.truth-out.org/opinion/item/18133-when-schools-become-dead-zones-of-the-imagination-a-critical-pedagogy-manifesto>. Diane Ravitch invokes Huxley's *Brave New World* in her widely read blog "Why We Should Care about Galvanic Response Skin Bracelets" June 11, 2012, available at <http://dianeravitch.net/?s=galvanic+skin+response>.
6 Henry A. Giroux "Totalitarian Paranoia in the Post-Orwellian Surveillance State" Truthout.org February 10, 2014, available at <www.truth-out.org/opinion/item/21656-totalitarian-paranoia-in-the-post-orwellian-surveillance-state>.
7 Btihaj Ajana, *Governing through Biometrics: The Biopolitics of Identity* New York: Palgrave, 2013.
8 See Nicole Nguyen, "Chokepoint: Regulating US Student Mobility through Biometrics" *Political Geography* 46 (May 2015), 1–10; and Alexander Means, *Schooling in the Age of Austerity* New York: Palgrave, 2013.
9 See Pierre Bourdieu, "The Forms of Capital" (1986) in *Cultural Theory: An Anthology* Malden, MA: Wiley-Blackwell, 2011.
10 Kwek, ibid.
11 See, for example, Mark Achbar's film *The Corporation* (2005) and the scholarship of Juliet Schorr.
12 John Chubb and Terry Moe, *Liberating Learning* San Francisco: John Wiley and Sons, 2009.
13 This heading references Robin Truth Goodman, "The New Taylorism: Hacking at the Philosophy of the University's End" *Policy Futures in Education* 10(6) (December 2012), 665–73. Goodman criticizes how Mark Taylor's neoliberal techno-utopianism for higher education constitutes students as knowledge consumers for corporate benefit.
14 See Wayne Au, "Teaching under the New Taylorism: High-Stakes Testing and the Standardization of the 21st Century Curriculum" *Journal of Curriculum Studies* 43(1) (2011), 25–45.
15 Herbert Kliebard, *The Struggle for the American Curriculum, 1893–1958*, 3rd edition New York: Routledge, 2004.
16 E. Wayne Ross, "Clockwork: Taylorism and its Continuing Influence on Work and Schooling" in *Social Studies and Diversity Teacher Education* (ed. E. Heilman) New York: Routledge, 2010, 33–7.
17 Giroux, *Theory and Resistance*, 170.
18 Joao Rosa and Ricardo Rosa, *Pedagogy in the Age of Media Control* New York: Peter Lang Publishers, 2011; Donaldo Macedo et al., *Media Literacy: A Reader*

New York: Peter Lang Publishers, 2007; Jeffrey Nealon and Susan Giroux, *The Theory Toolbox* Lanham, MD: Rowman & Littlefield, 2011.

19 Jonathan Crary, *Suspensions of Perception: Attention, Spectacle, and Modern Culture* Cambridge: MIT Press, 2001, 13.

20 See William James, "Attention" in *The Principles of Psychology* (Volume 1 of 2), Boston, MA: Digireads.com Publishing, 2010, 280–1.

21 See for example, Walter Benjamin, "The Work of Art in the Age of Mechanical Reproduction" in *Illuminations* New York: Shocken, 1968, 239–41.

22 See the scholarly attention studies of Adam Gazzaley and David L. Strayer. See also Matt Richtel, *A Deadly Wandering: A Tale of Tragedy and Redemption in the Age of Attention* New York: William Morrow, 2014.

23 Bernard Stiegler, *Taking Care of Youth and the Generations* Stanford, CA: Stanford University Press, 2010.

24 Henry A. Giroux, *Dangerous Thinking in the Age of the New Authoritarianism* Boulder, CO: Paradigm Publishers, 2015, 166–7.

4

CORPORATE EDUCATIONAL REFORM AND THE MAKING OF THE NEW FORCED CONSUMPTION

Educational Technology and the Destruction of Teachers as Public Intellectuals

Introduction: The Ideology of Choice to the Reality of Forced Consumption

Since the 1980s, one of the central ideological tactics that the political right has used to justify the privatization, defunding, and denunciation of public schooling has been the demand for introducing consumer choice into public education. This move captures the public desire for local control and autonomy, delinks it from collectively determined educational policy, and links it instead to the individualized promise of elite commodity consumption and the sheen of consumerism. Academic journals have published tens of thousands of articles debating "school choice" while think tanks have churned out countless advocacy pieces. First the Republican party and more recently much of the Democratic party have embraced market-based school reforms, taking their cues from armies of heavily funded influence peddling organizations such as Democrats for Education Reform, American Legislative Exchange Committee (ALEC), and the network of right-wing think tanks such as Heritage, Hoover, and American Enterprise Institute (AEI).

The most widespread manifestation of market-based "choice" is the charter movement that continues to expand despite its failure to deliver what it promised: raised test scores and decreased costs. Despite their unpopularity, the more overt market-based choice schemes of vouchers and "neo-vouchers" (scholarship tax credits for private schooling) continue to expand. Such "choice" schemes do more than reframe collective goods as individual consumer goods—they also eradicate choices under the guise of choice. For example, once public community schools have been closed and replaced by charters, there is no longer the choice of using the neighborhood school. Nor is there the choice often of walking to school or avoiding a far commute. Once "choice" schemes are launched, parents are told they can "choose" from what is left but they are not told that they can choose a well-supported neighborhood school.

The ideology of school choice has crucially relied upon the neoliberal framing of public sector goods and services as hopelessly bureaucratically encumbered and incapable of improvement. In this view, the promise of injecting the magic of private sector efficiencies and markets is just the right medicine for the terminally ill public sector. While the ideology of applying private consumer choice to the public sector remains solidly in place, a new phenomenon is forming that runs diametrically opposed to the ideology of consumer choice but that serves the same end of eroding the public sphere while selling off the public school system to investors and the rich. Technology and media corporations have become major players usurping the role of teachers, administrators, parents, students, and the public in determining what is taught and learned in schools.

As neoliberal ideology has propagated a conception of the parent as liberated consumer of private services, the teacher has been positioned as needing to be ever more disciplined and controlled. From efforts to eradicate teachers' unions directly and through charter expansion, to replacing security with value added modeling, to blaming teachers for every conceivable educational and social problem in mass media, to imposing scripted lessons, to ramping up standardization of curriculum, to undermining teacher pay, there has been no shortage of teacher bashing in the last decades. The ideologies of consumer choice and worker discipline/ teacher bashing are integral to the right-wing project that aims to reimagine education as a private market.

In the neoliberal imaginary, the idealized competitive market stands as a powerful symbol of how entrepreneurial zeal joins with consumer preference and market competition to foster dynamism, innovation, and individual freedom. This can be found in the celebration of "creative destruction" or "churn" that is celebrated as creating a model of continuous educational improvement. Charter schools or private voucher schools are opened, succeed and flourish or fail and "go out of business." While there is little evidence to suggest that the opening and closure of charter and voucher schools corresponds with educational quality traditionally defined (and plenty of negative evidence about various dimensions of both of these market schemes), there is an enormous disjuncture between the celebration of competitive markets and the tendency of markets towards monopoly. For example, there is a steady consolidation of educational management organizations. As Chris Whittle explained to the AEI in 2009, the dream is of a small number of massive education corporations dominating school provision globally in 25 years. Whittle's own Edison Schools, renamed Edison Learning, was premised on monopolistic proportions of growth for its success. In the narrative that lured investors, to be profitable the company had to achieve "economies of scale" to be one of the biggest school "districts" and have better purchasing power. As I detailed in my book *The Edison Schools,* the dream of "economies of scale" failed. Part of why it failed is simply that a model organized around skimming profits out of educational resource provision cannot in the end make up for the loss of resources through efficiencies. More broadly, as David Berliner and Gene Glass have shown, there is little evidence to suggest that the competition between charters and public schools exists at all.[1] But I want to consider here another fallacy of alleged educational competition and choice. That is, as large media corporations expand their reach and role as creators of curriculum and purveyors of educational technology products, they are claiming to expand teacher autonomy while they are in fact usurping the traditional role of teachers to control curriculum and pedagogy while also undermining the public democratic potential of teachers to act as public intellectuals.

In what follows here, I focus on two of the largest and most significant examples of the corporate hijacking of teaching from teachers and education professors through the use of for profit technology. The first section discusses the rise of educational hardware and software "tablet" products that are being produced and aggressively marketed by large media corporations such as News Corp, Apple, Microsoft, and Pearson NCS. I focus on how educational technology displaces teacher autonomy over pedagogical and curricular decisions while promoting approaches to education that reduce dialogue and reasoned inquiry while foreclosing the possibility of critical pedagogical practices. The second section discusses Pearson NCS's takeover of teacher education student teaching evaluation in the form of edTPA. edTPA is being used by 34 states. It requires students to be videotaped teaching, uploaded, and evaluated by a standardized rubric by anonymous reviewers at Pearson. The edTPA process displaces the tradition of education professors evaluating and discussing teaching practice with teacher candidates in person. Traditionally, such an evaluation was done in conjunction with university scholarship so that the clinical practice would be discussed in relation to educational scholarship. edTPA applies the logic of standardized testing to higher education but most significantly radically transforms the process of student teaching from one of reflective practice to one of staged performance. As in the previously discussed use of biometric pedagogy, edTPA employs technology to regulate, measure, and control teaching by targeting the bodies of teachers with surveillance. I conclude by discussing the importance of a reinvigorated movement for recognizing the role of the teacher as an engaged public intellectual against the trend of diminished teacher autonomy and deprofessionalization promoted by corporate reforms.

A Hard Tablet to Swallow: Corporate Technology and the Taking of the Class

Despite three decades of a mass media barrage denouncing public schools as failed and celebrating school privatization, most Americans trust public school teachers and schools in their communities and oppose school privatization and inadequate funding. The 2014 Phi Delta Kappan Annual Poll on public education reveals that the majority of Americans oppose both the Common Core Curriculum Standards and standardized testing because they undermine teachers' judgment and control over teaching and curriculum. Once again, Americans view their own local schools favorably and strongly favor control over schools to be held by local school councils rather than the state or federal government.[2] Yet, the direction of educational reform in the United States remains dominated by corporate interests that run counter to what most Americans value. Most notably, high stakes standardized testing and the push for the Common Core State Standards were put in place largely by the lobbying activities of large for profit publishing companies, especially McGraw Hill and Pearson NCS; vouchers and neo-vouchers (scholarship tax credits) have been expanded through the activities of Walmart money; and charters have been expanded through the relentless spending derived from Microsoft fortunes. Other media corporations, especially Apple and News Corp, have joined Microsoft in getting tablet computers and curriculum products into schools. The tech profiteers see tens of billions of dollars in contracting money there for the taking. The latest push for tech profiteering in schools was greased by the Common Core Curriculum Standards that was promoted by Gates and developed by Pearson. The Common Core allows for standardization and numerical quantification of knowledge. The ease of scoring public tax dollars for tech companies has been facilitated by an ideology of technophilia that equates technological progress with economic growth and human progress while misframing technology as outside of politics and ideology. This technophilia is interwoven with positivist ideology, a radical empiricism that suggests that all legitimate forms of learning must be numerically quantifiable and testable, that denies the role of subjectivity in the interpretation of facts, and that promotes a disingenuous and false objectivism with regard to the making of claims to truth. While the Common Core and its project of nationalizing high stakes standardized testing has taken a hit with the Every Student Succeeds Act and its shifting of testing to the states, the ideologies of technophilia and positivism are hardly dislodged by the latest reforms.

The largest players in the effort to hawk tablets and corporate curriculum to schools include Apple, Microsoft, and News Corp's Amplify. The potential for enormous sums of money is inspiring these monopolistic media firms to rush into classrooms. In 2013, Bill Gates predicted that in the next decade educational technology spending would be about a US$9 billion market.[3] The *Silicon Valley Business Journal* predicts educational technology spending in public schools to double to US$13.7 billion by 2017, propelled by the Common Core State Standards.[4] The signature Obama administration Race to the Top program, which aggressively promoted privatization and market-based reform, included in funds for North Carolina a US$30 million grant for educational technology. News Corp's Rupert Murdoch has openly discussed education in the United States as a US$500 billion dollar market.[5] Of course this is roughly the amount spent on all educational services annually in the United States. So when the mostly public spending on education is framed as a market, the idea of capturing that money in private service spending is presumed by profiteers such as Murdoch. The corporate commitment to education appears to be limited to its profit possibilities exemplified by News Corp's 2015 announcement that it intended to sell its education division Amplify! because it is not profitable enough.

The sale of Amplify!, which began as a purchase by News Corp of Wireless Generation, provides a reminder of the difference of commitment to education represented by public and private institutions. While public institutions ideally represent service to the public over the imperative for profit, private institutions maintain their commitment to the public only as long as it appears to its investors as maximally profitable relative to other opportunities. Private institutions oriented around maximizing short term financial gain bring the vicissitudes of markets into the public sector raising questions as to their reliability and stability over the long term.

Some of the largest early adoptions of tablet technology have made news for being stunning disasters. In North Carolina, which received that aforementioned US$30 million in Race to the Top (RTTT) funds, "The Guilford County public school district withdrew 15,000 Amplify tablets last fall. Pre-loaded with Common Core apps ... the devices peddled by News Corp. and Wireless Generation were rendered useless because of defective cases, broken screens, and malfunctioning power supplies."[6] Similarly the Los Angeles Unified School District spent US$1 billion dollars for overpriced Apple e-books that came with Pearson's Common Core branded apps. Students "breached the LAUSD's iPad firewalls and made a mockery of their adult guardians. Despite hefty investment in training and development, many teachers couldn't figure out how to sync up the tablets in the classroom."[7]

Some commentators in the popular press have pointed out that these contracting boondoggles need to be seen in relation to scarce public money for public schools as well as the gutting of entire areas of study such as the humanities in favor of test-prep-oriented forms of pedagogy and vocationally oriented curricula.[8] One critic on the far right, Michelle Malkin, who appears regularly on News Corp's Fox News, criticized the "EduTech Abyss" as symptomatic of big government overreach and wasteful spending on failed technology schemes. She criticizes the federal education machine and its wasteful spending on the Common Core State Standards that undermine local control. Here, ostensible criticism of the misuse of technology is part of a Tea Party diatribe against big government. Ultimately, Malkin expresses support for large government technology spending (read by her employers at News Corp), resorting to an argument that spans the political spectrum: what matters is efficacious implementation of technology in schools. What appears nearly universal in both the mass media and policy discussions of educational technology is an equation of the expansion of education technology with capitalist growth, the assumption that technology is a prerequisite for the proper formation of future potential workers and consumers, and that good teaching must utilize technology to be effective, and that even bad teaching can be made effective with technology. Technology is thoroughly wrapped up with a broader set of neoliberal educational assumptions and values including vocationalism, instrumentalism, school to work, privatization, and deregulation.

The neoliberal project of homogenizing and standardizing curricular content that can be mass produced and sold works compatibly with the neoconservative project of promoting a core or cannon of conservative knowledge.[9] Neoconservative cultural content such as Hirsch's Core Knowledge curriculum is at the center of the neoliberal K12, Inc. cyber homeschooling and charter school business. K12, Inc. remains the single largest for profit educational management company measured by number of students. As a business, K12, Inc. depends upon replacing teacher labor with technology, leaving classrooms of 50 students with a single teacher and technology facilitator. Predictably, studies of these "cyber-schools" show them having abysmal outcomes.[10]

Amplify's tablet technology is meant to capture scarce educational dollars that could be used to pay for more teachers to decrease class sizes. The tablets and the corporate curriculum are intended to become the basis for learning throughout the school day. As Anya Kamenentz writes, "Amplify presents a vision of an integrated, twenty-first century classroom—though it's also very much a corporate minded dream, in which one company provides every need."[11] In this corporate dream, the role of teachers and school administrators, parents and communities in deliberating about curriculum and pedagogy is replaced by corporate control of all aspects of the school. Standardization figures prominently in the project to decrease the single biggest expense in education: human labor. Technological automation in the form of learning analytics and mass produced curriculum programs stand to displace not only teachers but administrators as well. This is a corporate dream that its promoters falsely present as outside of politics.

Neoliberal education leader Joel Klein was a media executive and attorney for monopolistic media firm Bertelsmann, then public prosecutor going after Microsoft for monopolistic practices, then pro-privatization New York City Schools Chancellor, and then became the head of News Corp's Amplify division. Klein is explicit in denying the politics of knowledge and curriculum in Amplify's products: "Instead of relitigating the same fights about the workforce, accountability, and school choice, we're beginning to see a growing coalescence about the potential power of technology to empower teachers and engage kids." On the surface, Klein's technophilic doctrine of apolitical efficacy is hard to take seriously coming from a company, News Corp, that is the single largest global promoter of right-wing politics in mass media through *Fox News* and the *Wall Street Journal*. However, the suggestion that technology in schools has nothing to do with privatization (choice) and struggles over disciplining the teacher labor force is ludicrous. This is precisely what Amplify's technology products are about. They capture public money to be used in place of teacher work and displace the dialogue between teachers and students with prepackaged curricula to be consumed by students. They come loaded with curriculum products that have distinct ideologies, narratives, and ideas that represent particular points of view and group interests.

Neither technology nor the knowledge loaded onto its products is apolitical. As Istvan Meszaros explains, technology and science, despite being incessantly framed as the solution to environmental destruction, cannot on their own solve the problems they create:

> to say that "science and technology can solve all our problems in the long run" is much worse than believing in witchcraft; for it tendentiously ignores the devastating social embeddedness of present-day science and technology ... but whether we succeed in radically changing their direction, which is at present narrowly determined and circumscribed by the self-perpetuating needs of profit maximization.[12]

Public schools and the public sector more generally are targets for the class of people who own and control capital for accumulating profit. Technology products such as tablets and software products that the capitalist class sells to schools differ from the primary use of technology for business. As David Harvey explains:

> Capital's immediate purpose is to increase productivity, efficiency and profit rates, and to create new and, if possible, ever more profitable product lines. When considering the trajectories of technological change, it is vital to remember that the software and organizational forms are every bit as important as the hardware. Organizational forms, like the control structures of the contemporary corporation, the credit system, just-in-time delivery systems, along with the software incorporated into robotics, data management, artificial intelligence and electronic banking, are just as crucial to profitability as the hardware embodied in machines.[13]

As public schools are framed by investors, corporations, and tech companies as businesses, those organizational forms take greater prominence. Expansion of these technologies as "delivery systems" promotes both a transmissional model of pedagogy and the image of schooling as business. Of course, public schools do not exist to accumulate profit (although increasingly they are being privatized and commodified to do just that). They exist ostensibly to serve the public interest. However, that has been successfully redefined in neoliberal terms of opportunity for students to compete in the national and global capitalist economy towards the end of work and consumerism ("college and career readiness"). As Bowles and Gintis wrote in 1976 on the eve of the neoliberal onslaught:

> The system as it stands today provides eloquent testimony to the ability of the well-to-do to perpetuate in the name of equality of opportunity an arrangement which consistently yields to themselves disproportional advantages, while thwarting the aspirations and needs of the working people of the United States.[14]

In this individualized economic promise, technology plays an important symbolic role by being linked to capitalist growth, progress, and the technologized workplace of the imagined future. Technology education is interwoven with neoliberal false promises for individual upward mobility and the false promise that educational reform on its own can mitigate poverty, economic inequality, and a hierarchical class structure. If more education on its own is alleged to result in more income, opportunity, and consumption, then more technology education is alleged to result in even more market benefits.

Governments and corporations aggressively promote so-called STEM (science technology engineering mathematics) education in line with their assumptions of human capital theory. In the fantasy, every student will become an app developer, video game entrepreneur, or do some other tech work that requires little more than knowledge of how to code. Such economic promises that are alleged to result from STEM education disregard crucial aspects of what determines economic mobility for most, such as capital investment. The ideology of STEM for economic mobility has nothing to say about how in neoliberal globalization locally developed technologies have no reason to stay local in terms of their translation into commercial products and work opportunities. I work for the University of Massachusetts at Dartmouth, which has a technology emphasis and caters to working class students in the south of the state. Economically devastated cities in the region such as New Bedford and Fall River, which once had powerful textile industries, now have high unemployment, poverty, and a dwindling tax base as those textile industries now operate in the Pacific

Rim. Engineering graduates will pursue tech jobs outside the region near Cambridge or in Silicon Valley. There is little reason to believe that these dying cities will be able to recover as a consequence of investment in STEM. Yet, the rhetoric of STEM is used to justify K12 reform and frame policy issues especially through a neoliberal lens that equates tech industry with educational and labor opportunity. The point is not to suggest that there is no value in science, mathematics, and engineering education. The point is that these educational disciplines cannot be relied upon to save a locale from capital flight and the resulting unemployment, poverty, and social precarity. Social movements, political action, struggles to democratize institutions and expand the commons, and popular educative efforts to link local public problems to global justice aspirations stand a much better chance.[15]

Technologies of knowledge production in schools play a crucial social reproductive role in that they "preserve and promote the necessary mental conceptions of the world that facilitate productive activity, guide consumer choices and stimulate the creation of new technologies."[16] Indeed, aside from amassing wealth for the owners of media corporations, such as News Corp, the social reproductive role of the ideologies conveyed by and through technologies such as tablets and corporate curricula software programs are of primary importance in terms of their service to ruling class people. For example, there are ideological boundaries with regard to what can be taught and whose perspective can be taught in corporate-produced curriculum products. Corporations, like other institutions, do not commit suicide. Corporations are not going to produce knowledge and curriculum that calls into question the undemocratic social arrangements from which corporations and their owners benefit. Corporate curriculum will make narratives, histories, and perspectives that affirm rather than contest elite power, consumerism, "progress" understood through corporate stewardship, the corporate media monopoly, money driven elections, capitalism as the only imaginable economic system as opposed to economic democracy, representative forms of republican democracy rather than direct and participatory democracy, rarified views of culture rather than culture as contested, produced from below, and capable of transforming civil society, consciousness, and who holds power. In short, corporations will favor knowledge that represents the interests and perspectives of economic, political, and cultural elites at the expense of the interests and perspectives of workers, the poor, immigrants, women, and other historically oppressed people.

What kinds of social relations are fostered when teachers are replaced by tablets or other machines? What kinds of social relations are produced by replacing dialogue between students and teachers with students using touchscreen apps that are standardized in terms of their content and delinked from particular contexts and subjectivities of the student or the teacher? As Alex Means has explained, the rise of adaptive curriculum software is far from apolitical.[17] Adaptive learning software is like the movie streaming service Netflix. Netflix utilizes a program to predict the consumer's likely interest in particular films and consequently tailors what is readily available based in past selections. This builds a consumer identity profile based on the programmed assumptions of the software engineers as to what are the intelligible categories of film viewership. Of course, such categories are based in marketing and the interest in delivering inexpensively obtained content while retaining viewer subscriptions. Very different categories and suggestions would be developed if the aims were, for example, to promote viewership of films valued by and discussed by film scholars. Different aims and assumptions would result in a very different adaptive model.

Adaptive learning software changes the curriculum based on the test performance of the student. Consequently, it forms a case or identity profile of the student that then is used for sorting and sifting the student, determining capacities, interpreting intelligence and potential, and providing particular future curricula. As Zygmunt Bauman and David Lyons argue, what is at stake in the rise of surveillance technologies such as these is not only the loss of privacy and the expansion of secrecy for the wielding of unaccountable power but also the tendency towards *social sorting* and the making of "cumulative disadvantage."[18] What is particularly insidious about this new form of tracking is that it is wrapped in the ostensibly disinterested and objective guise of techno-science that naturalizes the outcomes of sorting as beyond human evaluation and judgment, free of assumptions and values, delinked from the vagaries of subjective all too human error. Of course, these software curricula are made by people with particular social positions, values, and ideologies and the content of the curricula expresses ideologies, values, and assumptions of particular classes and cultural groups.

One of the most significant political and pedagogical dimensions of the expansion of corporate tablet technology is the usurping of the role of the teacher by the corporation in making decisions about what and how to teach. The makers of tablet hardware and software curriculum claim that not only are they *not* usurping the roles of teachers but also they are actually expanding teacher autonomy and control in the classroom. Joel Klein, CEO of Amplify! claims that the tablet is not taking control from teachers but rather is simply responding to teachers' demands.[19] Anya Kamenentz describes the Amplify! software curriculum design that is alleged to give teachers control,

> many educators are still skeptical of tablets in the classroom—and Amplify seems designed to put them at ease. Its operating system gives teachers and schools an unprecedented level of control over the devices in students' hands. There is no HOME button, for example: Students can't just exist out of a math program the way they can close Angry Birds on an iPad. Instead, if a teacher hits her EYES ON TEACHER button, any or every student's tablet in her classroom suspends; a message tells the student to look up. Or the teacher can call on a student randomly, and a message pops up on her screen. Or with just one click, a teacher can pose a multiple-choice pop quiz and see instant results, set a five-minute timer for an activity, or divide students into discussion groups. Or she can automatically give individualized homework assignments based on the day's performance.[20]

Of course what the teacher does not control in these examples is the making, selecting, and administering of the curriculum itself nor the testing of that curriculum. The teacher does not put that math lesson up on the board, write that pop quiz, or engage in dialogue with the students about the object of knowledge. Instead, the teacher becomes a facilitator of prepackaged and standardized curriculum and assessments made by the company. In this case, technology takes the practice of scripted lessons a step further away from teacher control. Those individualized homework assignments are not the result of the teacher's decision-making and thought. Nor do they allow the student to comprehend knowledge and subjective experience critically, that is, in terms of the broader forces, structure, and material and symbolic contests informing their production. Rather, these assignments are the result of the learning analytic program that sorts students and makes the student into a case for future sorting.

Furthermore, as students use the prepackaged software, their scores are recorded and the data is managed from above the teacher for evaluation of the teacher's "performance." The teacher is caught in a data surveillance web in which control over the making of the knowledge with the student is replaced by automated measures of learning determined by the accounting practices installed in the machine.

Anya Kamenentz frames the problem of technology as a battle between total corporate control over knowledge and the school versus the use of technology for "open access" to freely accessible knowledge and curriculum. She asks education investor Matt Greenfield whether the Amplify! model of total integrated corporate control of the classroom will win out over the "open source" model. In the integrated model, a company such as News Corp seeks monopoly control over the integrated hardware product and proprietary software product. In the open source model, computer hardware such as laptops and tablets is left open for a variety of web-based applications such as Wikipedia or the curriculum software that a school or district develops itself. This, however, is a false dichotomy between future technology models. Once the technology is in the classroom, the public is beholden to it. That is, educational spending gets channeled towards acquiring, maintaining, and upgrading the hardware if not also the software. Such spending comes at the expense of decidedly low maintenance resources such as books that also more centrally rely upon the teacher.

Kamenentz and Greenfield frame the debate over the future of educational technology as between the Amplify! model of total corporate monopoly versus open source technology. This framing misses the crucial issue of the different capacities that different schools have for implementation. A monopolistic model such as Amplify! that controls hardware and curriculum means that not only do working class and poor schools get targeted for highly standardized and scripted forms of pedagogy and pre-packaged curricula but it also means that these cash strapped schools are beholden to high technology spending in place of such proven beneficial reforms as smaller class sizes. Classroom technologies crowd out critical pedagogies that relate learning to power, ethics, and politics.[21]

Some technologists position "open source" technology as a hopeful alternative in that technology allows schools to access Wikipedia or other information sources. Bill Gates, for example, celebrates the open source charter school Summit Public Schools for "building its own learning platform that is student driven."[22] It is easy to see the allure of open access technology, especially for leapfrogging over an historical failure to invest in books, libraries and pre-digital information forms. Hundreds of schools in Chicago have no libraries. Why invest in paper books? Schools in many African nations have no material resources and yet the population has wide access to cell phone technology. Open access technology projects paired with hardware seem to offer a promise of instantly creating access.

However, unless governments provide public schools access to a network of all public libraries, such "openness" is a false promise from the start in that it will simply replicate the market driven, tiered access model of the subscription-based for profit publishing industry. For example, there is a radical difference in the access to library information and databases between elite universities and third tier universities. Worse, if the subscription model is abandoned in favor of a commercial advertising-driven model of "open source," public schooling collapses into the commercial culture of advertising-saturated television and internet. Furthermore, a pattern of targeting working class and poor urban and rural schools for repressive pedagogical approaches and standardized curricula appears to be continuing in the ways that these two approaches, vertical integration and open access, are being discussed. High degrees of bodily control, discipline, and standardization have a historical legacy intertwined with efforts to make poor students and non-White students docile and compliant for exploitative work and for assent to political marginalization. Students have also become increasingly valuable for short term profit as they are commodities in for profit schooling contracting and privatization schemes. As Alex Molnar and Faith Boninger have shown, technological forms of school commercialism are on the rise.[23]

Perhaps most pertinent here is the question of how different schools and students have different capacities to make curriculum within the open access model. It is crucial for students and teachers not simply to default to using whatever preexisting curricula are readily available. Instead, to be involved in making knowledge, teachers and students need both the material resources and critical intellectual tools to do so.

If Amplify!'s monopolistic design is about more tightly controlling and displacing teacher labor, it is also deeply in line with the trend to more tightly control student bodies as expressed by the repressive pedagogies found in KIPP, the discourse of grit, biometric pedagogy, and the use of smart drugs. Amplify! sells its hardware by promoting teacher control in the form of its One Click feature that freezes the computer screens of the students. It also sells tablets with the promise of being technologically relevant, "Among the features of Amplify's digital curriculum is the ability for teachers to see if students really understand vocabulary words when they use them in Twitter-like hashtags and other social media contexts."[24] Aside from the dubious pedagogical benefits of such innovations there is a basic question as to why would anyone want to teach comprehension of vocabulary through the most limiting of social media formats like Twitter rather than through intellectual traditions, interpretation of texts, literature, and essays that convey ideas while teaching dispositions of interpretation and judgment. Amplify's approach seems to belie a kind of formalism in which allegedly catchy media formatting becomes the basis for learning. Amplify seems to aim to be stylistically and technologically relevant rather than meaningful to students in ways that would help them understand themselves, understand how social forces make them as selves, to develop a language to name and comprehend themselves and the world, and to develop a sense of the capacity to act with others to control and transform their life conditions. In other words, the basic limitation of these technology products is that their degree of standardization, homogenization, and displacement of the role of the teacher actively prohibits forms of engagement aimed at reconstructing experience and fostering political rather than merely consumer agency.

edTPA and the Evacuation of the Educational Scholar and Dialogue from Student Teaching

The rise of edTPA, a national standardized teacher performance assessment, shares the logic of politicized forced consumption through the use of technology as well as the broader tendency to undermine critical forms of education. edTPA is a high stakes exit exam for teacher candidates. A number of states have made passage of edTPA a prerequisite for state licensure, and a number of states are in the process of implementing it for that purpose. According to its designers and most vocal defenders, which include Stanford education professor Linda Darling-Hammond and University of Minnesota education professor Mistilina Sato, edTPA was created as part of an effort to defend teacher education as a professional endeavor akin to law and medicine. Darling-Hammond and Sato compare the test to board examinations. edTPA is significant for seeking to standardize clinical teaching assessment nationally. It is also significant for removing the evaluation of student teaching candidates from the context of the student teaching. It replaces dialogic forms of assessment between education professors and teacher candidates with review of teaching by an anonymous reviewer unfamiliar with the candidate, the school, the students, and the context. Test takers videotape themselves teaching a sample lesson in a classroom and upload the lesson through Pearson's edTPA website. The test costs teacher candidates US$300 and US$100 for each retest. Pearson pays anonymous scorers US$75 to grade the candidate's video using a standardized rubric.

edTPA has rightly been criticized by critical scholars Julie Gorlewski and Barbara Madeloni for its rejection of the significance of contexts from the teaching process, for presuming that teaching that is of value must be measurable and numerically quantifiable, for standardizing and narrowing what counts as good teaching, for treating teaching as a performance in which there is a definitive sense of what counts as good teaching that is beyond dispute, argumentation, or debate.[25] Gorlewski and Madeloni also emphasize that "part of our work (as teachers) is to explore the ideologies and values hidden in the 'practical' aspects of teaching by examining underlying assumptions about learning, motivation, and the purpose of schooling."[26] As they put it, edTPA "invades this experience" by marshaling students towards preparing to meet the test requirements "at the expense of realizing when they are making value-based ideological choices."[27] They suggest that teacher candidates in teacher education programs change how they approach coursework and student teaching to follow the rubrics that form the basis for the scoring and that the scoring "operate[s] in the realm of 'value-free' language" to pursue passage. Of course, language is never free of underlying values, assumptions, and ideologies. Gorlewski and Madeloni emphasize that edTPA pushes to the background critical forms of teaching and learning that prepare teachers to analyze, comprehend, and engage with the values, assumptions, and ideologies that undergird teaching practice. Instead, they contend, teacher education courses are transformed by edTPA. It displaces student concerns with critical forms of teaching and learning with class time and student focus on students' concern with fulfilling the high stakes test rubrics.

One of the designers of the edTPA, Mistilina Sato, published an article in the *Journal of Teacher Education,* a publication of the American Association of Colleges of Teacher Education (AACTE). AACTE is a major promoter of edTPA. The article "What is the Underlying Conception of Teaching in the edTPA?" addresses criticisms of the test, such as those from the critical perspective represented by Madeloni and Gorlewski. Sato defends the exit exams as necessary for "professional" standards. She suggests that critics of the test are mistaken in their criticisms because even though edTPA insists on "identifiable learning outcomes" and it "does narrow the outcomes for students to quantifiable measures of learning" and "the focus on content learning outcomes narrows the conception of teaching to one that emphasizes disciplinary learning,"[28] theoretically, there is nothing in the edTPA that prohibits a teacher candidate from employing critical pedagogy. "The teacher candidate selects the learning goal and the means by which the student learning is evaluated."[29] Learning outcomes such as "personal growth," "self-actualization," or "humanistic aims" are not "prohibited" but are also not treated as outcomes but rather "supports" for "the core focus of the edTPA as an assessment of successful or competent teaching."[30] "Thus, a conception of teaching as transformative … is not the core conception underpinning the edTPA."[31]

Sato affirms the core conception of the edTPA as "content learning" that "emphasizes disciplinary learning."[32] She writes, "There is a clear expectation that the act of 'teaching' leads to an identifiable learning outcome for students."[33] Despite the profession of an openness to what she calls "critical pedagogy," Sato's discussion clarifies several crucial differences between what edTPA promotes and critical pedagogy. The underlying conception of teaching in the edTPA through "disciplinary based" "content learning" is that learning goals are "defined and aligned with local, state, or national standards," leading precisely to what Freire described as banking education, despite Sato's assertion to the contrary. The very framing of knowledge as "content" presumes a delivery or transmission model of pedagogy that denies the educative process in knowledge making. It also denies, more importantly, the fact that knowledge is struggled over by different groups and individuals with often incommensurable material and symbolic interests. The suggestion that disciplinary knowledge (subject knowledge) needs to be transmitted and justified through state standards in this way likewise treats the disciplines in their state sanctified form as beyond question and beyond the question of who precisely formed the disciplines and whose knowledge, values, and ideologies are represented by the disciplines. This is not an argument against the study of traditions of thought nor is it an argument against government involvement in learning standards and curricular oversight. It is an argument for the ruthless interrogation of those traditions and for states to embrace the reflective traditions of critical education.

At the core of critical pedagogy, for example, is a recognition that learning is interwoven with power struggles and contests between different classes and cultural groups. Both knowledge and experience in the practice of critical pedagogy need to be relentlessly questioned in terms of what authorizes claims to truth and how seemingly natural experiences are anything but innocent. To put it differently, critical pedagogy involves a process of questioning how objective forces, structures, and systems produce students' experiences and structure their subjectivity. As well, critical pedagogy involves a process of learning to theorize, interpret, and judge both experience and new knowledge in order to act on and shape the broader objective social world. For critical pedagogy, learning and knowledge become the basis for political agency, but this all becomes impossible if knowledge is treated as "content" and bounded by the "disciplines" and if "good" teaching is about efficiently or inefficiently "delivering" this "content" through a videotaped performance.

Sato mischaracterizes the project of critical pedagogy as "social reform" and evacuates from her discussion of critical pedagogy the crucial concepts of power, agency, and the constitutive antagonisms structuring both the social and the individual. Critical pedagogy is a project of social and individual transformation in which the goal is the vocation of becoming more fully human and creating a society free of domination and exploitation. Yet, the edTPA is a project of control that necessarily aims to delink learning from the class and cultural struggles over knowledge and meaning-making practices. It does so through a liberal lens of consensus about what constitutes knowledge and the "disciplines," and it conceals its authoritarian bent through a guise of methodological flexibility. Teacher candidates can teach whatever they want as long as they justify it in terms of layers of government standards and unexamined disciplines. What Sato fails to address is that edTPA does not just promote forms of learning which evacuate the necessarily social and political aspects of knowledge, teaching, and learning but it also promotes particular forms of subjectivity defined through submission to authority, rule following, a preoccupation with learning as fulfilling a rubric made by someone else, surveillance and the evacuation of dialogue.

As Stuart Hall and Henry Giroux have emphasized, culture is formed through unequal dialogic exchange. Subjects are formed in and through culture, and culture has a pedagogical and political formative dimension. Culture provides not just knowledge and meanings but also subject positions and points of identification. edTPA needs to be recognized as ritual practice that involves learning to think of teaching as something that is performed for an unseen power with whom one cannot discuss or question the practice. It transforms teacher preparation from being a process of thinking, questioning, and reflection upon action with the use of theory from courses and dialogue with mentors to being one of deciphering the cues of the rubrics to prepare a performance designed to "please the gods," the unseen reviewer.

Specifically, the edTPA replaces the dialogue and reflective practice between a teacher candidate and a teacher educator that would form the basis for reflection upon the student's teaching practice. Instead, the use of the videotape uploaded onto the Pearson website, to be judged by the absent reviewer, makes meaningful dialogue about the teaching practice no longer a part of the evaluation of student teachers. Consequently, teaching is not just transformed into a scripted performance based in the anticipated standardized judgment of the invisible reviewer but it is also rendered a one way monological act. edTPA brings what Foucault detailed as normalizing judgment and hierarchical surveillance, the logic of the examination broadly conceived, into the practice of student teaching. The student teacher is judged, compared, homogenized, and hierarchically evaluated with reference to a norm by an unseen seer.

Good teaching fosters curiosity, creativity, sustained inquiry, dispositions for dialogue and dissent and not only for asking and framing questions but also for learning to make reasoned thoughtful interpretations and judgments. Good teaching involves helping students comprehend how different claims to truth and interpretations are informed by broader social, political, and cultural realities.

The social and individual cost of the expansion of edTPA is the development of forms of teacher education that deny the relationships between knowledge and student experience and deny the relationships between knowledge and broader objective forces and realities. edTPA fails to account for how the process of learning is always wrapped up with the ways objective forces form subjects pedagogically and how subjects produce and struggle over knowledge. In the course of learning, knowledge can be reconstructed, mediated, and theorized to be the basis for new understanding and forms of agency to act on and shape social realities. In its denial of the political dimensions of learning, edTPA is a highly politicized examination that aims foremost to structure time, space, and knowledge in ways that shut down critical questions and approaches to teaching and learning. edTPA marshals teachers-in-the-making towards teaching that is concerned with "curricular alignment," following standards, delivering knowledge made by experts elsewhere, and avoiding "dangerous" questions about the relationships between learning, knowledge, and the social world.

edTPA is justified by proponents as necessary to defend academic forms of teacher education against corporate reformers who would privatize teacher preparation and strip it from the purview of academia. This is a serious concern as venture philanthropists such as Gates, Broad, and Walton and the recent Every Student Succeeds Act are aggressively working to privatize both teacher and leader preparation. Some on the left such as Wayne Au have accepted this justification and embraced edTPA as the lesser evil than allowing the corporate dismantling agenda to win.[34] Au suggests that educators on the left ought to embrace edTPA as a legitimate part of claiming teaching as a profession—a defense of teacher education made by liberals such as Linda Darling-Hammond. The professionalization agenda brings together a comparison of teaching to other professions and claims the need for rigorous professional standards. As I argued in *The Gift of Education,* the "professionalization agenda" for teacher education is itself a deeply class-based politicized framing for teacher education. Part of what is wrong with the professionalization agenda is that it suggests a profoundly and impossibly depoliticized view of education—this is a liberal view that Au's critical scholarship consistently challenges. Consider the professionalization agenda in contrast with, for example, Henry Giroux's call for teachers to be transformative intellectuals in the tradition of Antonio Gramsci.[35] Giroux's position recognizes the distinction between teachers as traditional intellectuals who make knowledge in the service of economic and political elites and teachers as transformative intellectuals who make knowledge in the service of the people. In this view, knowledge-making activity is never innocent and never outside of broader structures, material and symbolic struggles, and antagonisms.

What is ultimately at stake in the battle over the use of technology in teaching is the contest between, on the one hand, education driven by the market ideology of consumer choice and neoliberal technophilia and, on the other hand, forms of education that create the conditions for people to control their lives as critically engaged public citizens in a democracy. The latter demands that technology serves the public interest and that the uses of technology in teaching be animated foremost by the role of the teacher as a public intellectual committed to democratic social transformation in all domains.

Notes

1 See David Berliner and Gene Glass, *50 Myths and Lies that Threaten America's Public Schools* New York: Teachers College Press, 2014.

2 "The PDK/Gallup Poll of the Public's Attitude toward Public Schools" Part I September 2014 and Part II October 2014, available at <http://pdkintl.org/noindex/PDK_Poll46_2014.pdf>.

3 Anya Kamenetz, "News Corp's Big Test" Fast Company.Com July August 2013, 43.

4 Michelle Malkin, "Feeding the Edu-Tech Beast" *Pittsburgh Tribune,* January 13, 2014.

5 Kamenetz, 43.

6 Malkin, ibid.

7 Malkin, ibid.

8 Malkin, ibid.

9 Michael Apple, *Educating the Right Way* New York: Routledge, 2006.

10 See for example, Stephanie Simon, "Cyber Schools Flunk, but Tax Money Keeps Flowing" *Politico*, September 25, 2013, available at <www.politico.com/story/2013/09/cyber-schools-flunk-but-tax-money-keeps-flowing-97375.html>.

11 Kamenentz, ibid. 43.

12 Istvan Meszaros, *The Necessity of Social Control* New York: Monthly Review Press, 2015, 29.

13 Harvey, *Seventeen Contradictions and the End of Capitalism*, 92

14 Bowles and Gintis, *Schooling in Capitalist America*, 30.

15 We take this up in Noah Delissovoy, Alex Means, and Kenneth Saltman, *Toward a New Common School Movement* Boulder, CO: Paradigm, 2014.

16 Harvey, *Seventeen Contradictions and the End of Capitalism*, 100.

17 Alexander J. Means "Algorithmic Education, Big Data, and the Control Society: Toward a Decolonial and Biotechnical Commons" *Cultural Studies in Science Education* (in press).

18 Zygmunt Bauman and David Lyon, *Liquid Surveillance* Malden, MA: Polity Press 2013, 13–14.

19 Bloomberg LP, *CQ Roll Call* "Amplify CEO Joel Klein Interviewed on Bloomberg TV" April 4, 2014.

20 Kamenentz, ibid., 43.

21 It was unsurprising to me that Kamanetz framed out crucial questions of power and specifically the cultural politics of knowledge with regard to technology and school reform. She interviewed me at length for her book *The Test: Why Our Schools are Obsessed with Standardized Testing but You Don't Have to Be* and excluded from her discussion any mention of the points I made to her about the way testing denies the values, knowledge, assumptions, and ideologies behind competing claims to truth and the inevitable connections between particular knowledge and the material and symbolic interests of individuals and groups. She clearly understood and was familiar with these ideas but, as most journalists who want to rise in the field, appears to accept the ideological limits of popular journalism and avoided raising the dangerous questions.

22 Kamenentz, ibid., 43.

23 Alex Molnar and Faith Boninger, *On the Block: Student Data and Privacy in the Digital Age—The Seventeenth Annual Report on Schoolhouse Commercializing Trends, 2013–2014*. Boulder, CO: National Education Policy Center, 2015. Retrieved from <http://nepc.colorado.edu/publication/schoolhouse-commercialism-2014>.

24 Motoko Rich, "New All-Digital Curriculums Hope to Ride High-Tech Push in Schoolrooms" *The New York Times* March 3, 2014, A13.

25 Barbara Madeloni and Julie Gorlewski, "Wrong Answer to the Wrong Question: Why We Need Critical Teacher Education not Standardization" *Rethinking Schools* 27(4) (2013), 16–21.

26 Madeloni and Gorlewski, ibid.

27 Madeloni and Gorlewski, ibid.
28 Mistilina Sato, "What is the Underlying Conception of Teaching of the edTPA?" *Journal of Teacher Education* 65(5) (2014), 421–34, 426.
29 Sato, ibid. 426.
30 Sato, ibid. 426.
31 Sato, ibid. 426.
32 Sato, ibid. 426.
33 Sato, ibid. 426.
34 Wayne Au, "What's a Nice Test like You Doing in a Place like This?: The edTPA and Corporate Education Reform" *Rethinking Schools* 27(4) (2013), 22–7, available online at <www.rethinkingschools.org/archive/27_04/27_04_au.shtml>.
35 Henry Giroux, *Teachers as Intellectuals* Westport, CT: Bergin & Garvey, 1988.

5

LEARNING TO BE A PSYCHOPATH

The Pedagogy of the Corporation

In the prior chapters, I have discussed how students' minds and bodies have become a locus of control for corporate profit and a target for the ideologies of corporate culture. I have shown how corporations have successfully cornered the market in selling points of identification so that student subjectivities are lured into identifying with a neoliberal corporate climate. In this chapter, I look at the development of this corporate point of identification—that is, what is it that students identify with when they identify with the corporation?

In his book and film *The Corporation* (2005), Joel Bakan suggests that since the corporation is legally treated as a human person, then we ought to ask: exactly what kind of person is the corporation?[1] His answer: a psychopath. Bakan points to the key characteristics shared by psychopaths and corporations including: disregard for the well-being of others, a lack of conscience, coldly calculated self-interested behavior, and grandiosity. Psychiatry classifies psychopaths as suffering from "anti-social personality disorder."[2] For Bakan, corporations behave in anti-social ways by being legally obligated to maximize shareholder profit in any way possible within the bounds of the law.

An oil corporation makes a calculated decision to squeeze extra profit by risking the destruction of an ocean. An automotive corporation saves six dollars per human death by not recalling a part that explodes in a crash because the insurance payouts are cheaper than the recall. A news corporation tells lies on a news program about the proven cancer risks of growth hormone in milk to please advertisers and maximize advertising revenue.

A business machine manufacturer does business with a fascist war enemy. A fruit company uses wealth and influence to overthrow a democratically elected government in favor of a military dictatorship. The examples are endless.[3] As Bakan contends, corporate personhood and limited liability are only held in place by human-made laws that could be changed to give priority to the public interest over corporate profit. People who are psychopaths have, according to Jared DeFife, clinical psychology research scientist and associate director of the Laboratory of Personality and Psychopathology, "a certain set of personality traits that includes emotional shallowness, superficial charm, impulsivity with poor judgment, deceitfulness, unreliability, manipulation, and disregard for the feelings (and well-being) of others."[4] Likewise, corporations externalize the social costs of their profit-motivated activities with little regard for the human consequences.

Corporations invest elaborately in superficially charming consumers with fantastic associations between products and a dreamworld of consumption.[5] Corporate leaders are required to make fast if not impulsive, egoistic decisions that are always dictated by an interpretation of what will best serve the bottom line. Corporations keep their financial dealings, intentions, and strategies hidden from the public, and, when confronted, frequently employ deception to evade responsibility for destructive acts and to compete in the marketplace. Such deception includes the systematic use of corporate spies and contracted disinformation campaigns. Corporations produce an image of themselves as reliable and stable, rational and benevolent, and yet will fire thousands of workers, discontinue a product or parts, aggressively lobby for socially destructive deregulations, or offshore production with no notice at all. Corporations are master manipulators and hire professional manipulators and propagandists in the public relations, advertising, and influence industries to achieve their aims. As Bakan rightly argues, corporate psychopathology is not mitigated either by corporate social responsibility efforts or by virtuous individuals being in their employ. Ultimately, corporations are legally beholden to shareholders to maximize profit by any means necessary. Corporations may do altruistic or "socially responsible" projects but only if they contribute to expanding profit and not if it threatens profits. Hence, corporate codes of social responsibility do not compensate for a systemic tendency for externalizing destruction onto the public. The ineffectiveness of voluntary ethical codes is particularly glaring in the sweatshop, oil, and beverage industries as socially destructive practices recur as soon as media attention wanes.[6] Nor can corporate behavior be understood as being reliant upon the virtues and goodwill of particular corporate leaders. The leading scholar on psychopaths, Bob Hare, who created the most widely used diagnostic test for psychopathy (the psychopath test), contends that psychopaths are over-represented four-fold relative to the general population in the ranks of business leadership.[7] Hare's perspective complements Bakan's in that both presume that the traits necessary for success for individuals in the business corporation are the same as the traits that define the institution.

Popular discourse about psychopaths is usually funneled through sensationalist scare stories and true crime tabloid television. On the other hand, the scholarly discourse can be found divided into three types:

I. Biological Determinism

Hare's checklist alleges to identify psychopaths through a survey, and it has come to be widely used in prisons and parole hearings to keep incarcerated those who score highly. Scientific study of psychopathology has tended to focus on brain science and in particular differences in amygdala function in psychopaths and non-psychopaths as a way of explaining the absence of empathy for others.[8] MRI studies purport to show that the brains of the two groups respond differently when shown grisly violent images: non-psychopaths fire up with activity for fear and stress while psychopaths register pleasure. The assumption throughout much of the scientific literature is that psychopathology is a function of broken biology which, if understood, could be potentially cured through surgical or pharmacological intervention. This is a view in which behavior can be read off of biology—a view consistent with socio-evolutionary biology and conservative strains of biopolitics in US political science.[9] While some researchers claim that cognitive behavioral therapy, a kind of reward–punishment behaviorist conditioning approach, is effective for curbing the violence of psychopathic youth, this treatment largely affirms an assumption of biological determinism.[10]

II. A Location for Psychopaths: The Corporation

The second group of academic views focuses on how psychopaths gravitate to professions that reward traits such as ruthlessness, egotism, a lack of empathy, grandiosity, and predatory tendencies. Most of this literature is concerned with the disproportionate representation of psychopaths in business and specifically in corporate leadership roles. Bob Hare himself has contributed to this literature with his book *Snakes in Suits*, co-authored with Paul Babiak, and an Australian scholar, Clive R. Boddy, has cornered the market in academic journal articles that seek to explain corrupt and unethical business practice through the presence of psychopaths in corporations. Unlike Bakan, these authors do not recognize the psychopathic dimensions of the institution of the corporation. In fact, rooting out psychopaths in the ranks of the corporations becomes a convenient explanatory device consistent with the "bad apples" alibi of neoliberal deregulatory destruction. If only there were no "bad-apple" corporate leaders such as Ken Lay and scam artists like Bernard Madoff, then the system would work ethically. Of course, neoliberal deregulation set the stage for the entire finance industry to create rip-off products and tank the system, requiring public bailout for survival. British journalist Ron Jonson's popular book *The Psychopath Test* reached a broader audience through NPR's public radio program *This American Life* which did an episode on psychopaths organized around Jonson's book. Both the book and the radio program focus on a notoriously cut-throat CEO of several companies including Sunbeam, Al Dunlap, whose management success was oriented around cost cutting by firing masses of employees. According to Jonson, Dunlap's home is adorned with statues of predatory animals with whom he identifies, and he recounts the extreme pleasure Dunlap takes in giving employees the axe. The literature on the corporate psychopath shares with the biologically deterministic perspective the assumption that psychopaths are born not made.

III. Culturalism

One article, "Deconstructing the Psychopath: A Critical Discursive Analysis," stands out in suggesting that the identity category of the psychopath is a social and historical construction.[11] This familiar Foucauldian argument suggests that the biological uniqueness of the psychopath consists in arbitrary physical traits that are made the basis for cultural norming through the expert discourses of medicine and psychology. In this view, there really are no such people as psychopaths, only deeds attributed to this fictive category. What is more, to be a psychopath is to be spoken of and, hence, produced as a psychopathic subject.

Pedagogy of the Psychopath

Just as the biologically deterministic perspective leaves no way to link the physically distinct traits of the psychopath to historically contingent cultural patterns of behavior and affect, the culturally deterministic approach allows for no capacity to comprehend the biology of psychopathy. Moreover, the biological deterministic, culturally deterministic, and "locational" approaches to the psychopath all miss a key aspect to the psychopath that I seek to redress here: psychopath culture is taught and learned—that is, it is pedagogical. The traits of the psychopath are not merely rewarded by certain institutions such as business schools and corporate headquarters. They are also broadly promoted on, for example, reality television programs which celebrate a social Darwinian ethos, calculated betrayal, exclusionary forms of sociality, and cruelty.[12]

This chapter expands Bakan's question from one of asking what kind of person the corporation is (a psychopath) to asking what sorts of persons the corporation educates flesh and blood persons into becoming—not only inside corporations but also how corporations are involved in educating the public in a number of ways. Perhaps the greatest force that corporations wield is cultural pedagogical. That is, corporations, and particularly media corporations, produce narratives, ideologies, and identifications that form the basis of identities. The pedagogies of the corporation form points of identification from which individuals draw to interpret, act on, and intervene in the social world. Corporate educational projects can be found in formal schooling in the form of school commercialism initiatives, such as BP's involvement with creating California's science curriculum; museum education projects, such as Monsanto's sponsorship of "Underground Adventure" a permanent exhibit on earth and agriculture at the Field Museum in Chicago; or ExxonMobil's heavy spending to promote public school privatization.[13] Literature such as detective and crime fiction, television, and film also function as cultural pedagogues.[14] In what follows here I focus on and contrast two very different pedagogical and political interventions on the psychopath, Patricia Highsmith's Ripley novels and George Manos' *Dexter* television series. I focus on these texts in part to emphasize the extent to which cultural producers affirm or contest broader public discourses, ethical and political positions. Such meaning-making practices create the formative culture and common sense values, assumptions, and ideologies with which youth and adults learn to interpret, judge, and act on the world they inhabit.

While the psychopathic character has long taken shape as a cartoonish villain in innumerable films and television shows, only recently has the psychopath appeared as a popular or heroic protagonist in mass media. Patricia Highsmith's Ripley novels and Jim Thompson's crime fiction from the 1950s provide an exploration of social life narrated by psychopathic selves. While offering identification with a violent psychopath protagonist, these novels do not celebrate or endorse the amorality they represent, nor do they suggest the virtue for society in universalizing psychopathic traits. Detective fiction by Robert B. Parker (Spencer series 1970s–2010) and Walter Mosley (1990s–2000s) both have black psychopathic outlaws who periodically must be relied upon to kill for the heroic detective, breaking the law in order to uphold the detective's pursuit of justice which the law of the state fails to provide.

More recently television shows ranging from gamecon reality TV to *24*, *Dexter*, and numerous action films suggest that psychopathic traits such as remorselessness, brutality, and disregard for the well-being of others are no longer characteristic of the social outsider. Instead, these corporate traits are framed as necessary for survival in a neoliberal Darwinian social sharktank, defending the dominant order and harnessing violence and lawlessness in the service of a conservative morality. These anti-heroics of the contemporary psychopath share an affinity with an upwardly redistributive economic policy climate as well as with the political "state of exception" that has expanded since 9/11 and that is used to justify state murder and other lawbreaking outside of international and domestic law. Such exceptions are typified by targeted assassination, the rejection of habeas corpus, the USA Patriot Act, rash environmental exploitation, the expropriation of public properties for private exploitation through the recent transformations to eminent domain, and NSA spying on the public. The crucial issue here is that recent narratives of the psychopath have not merely *responded to* a radically transformed and allegedly ethically ambiguous post-9/11 political, economic, and cultural climate. Rather, these narratives have actively participated in producing an acceptability and celebration of psychopath politics and culture. More specifically, these narratives have promoted a deeply authoritarian version of anti-democratic justice through the making of the psychopath as a point of identification for the just agent. *Dexter* writer James Manos, Jr. (Howard, 2010: 19–20) joins *Dexter* creator Shawn Ryan in asking the question, "What would people be willing to accept for their own safety?"(Howard, 2010: 23). (In other words, are people willing to accept a publicly unaccountable secret police force of murderers privately enforcing a security agenda?) Recent narratives of the psychopath produced by cultural workers including Manos and Ryan have participated in *re-educating the public* to a revised conception of justice in which the vigilante exceptionalism of the psychopath displaces the law of the state.

Although endless fictional and journalistic television programs since the 1970s have ramped up the specter of the psychopathic killer to redefine public space and community as dangerous, *Dexter* in particular stands out in popular culture for making the psychopath an agent of justice. As dominant ideology, the threat of the violent monster lurking among us has served as a means to sell advertising through spectacular violence. News coverage of mass killers and mass shooting events overtake both political and economic news events with spectacular narratives where the killers are at first depicted as pinnacles of seeming normalcy to their neighbors only to take a tragic, terrifying turn, making it seem that anybody could turn a gun on the crowds, even the most seemingly unlikely and soft-spoken suspect. Such programming at the same time promotes a conservative ideology of state violence. In the camera obscura of state violence, its real primary aim of protecting private property rights and relations for elites appears instead as protection of everybody from the ever-present threat of pathological violence from deranged killers and child molesters.

The recent elevation of the violent psychopath to heroic stature coincides with an economic moment in which capitalist reproduction requires fewer workers, greater inequalities in wealth and income, a concentration of wealth at the top, and the expansion of a disposable segment of people at the bottom. As Michele Byers has pointed out, Dexter offers identification with a neoliberal subject of capacity achieving justice for the failed public sector.[15] The figure of the heroic psychopath appears at a time when the United States can be easily described, as Charles Ferguson does, as a Predator Nation in which deregulation of public controls over finance and the private sector joins with radical upward redistributions in not just wealth and income but also control over public priorities and government. With both political parties thoroughly under the sway of corporate money and committed to neoliberal privatization and deregulation in every area from education to housing to healthcare, politics has been transformed into a matter of the capture of public money and pillage of resources. In such a climate of social exclusion and atrophied opportunity, the promise of success and power appeals to the ordinary American through identification with a figure that promises exceptional and extraordinary power, freed of the burden of conscience and empathy for others, the ultimate predator.

This image covers over the fact that the same ordinary American is the target of extremely painful economic and political policy. To put it differently, the individual identifies with the corporate psychopath that she is the target of.

I identify the rise of the psychopathic character as a recent heroic figure in popular culture and particularly in popular fiction, television, and film perhaps best typified by the television show *Dexter*. Patricia Highsmith's Ripley novels prefigured the themes found in *Dexter*, including a protagonist without a conscience or guilt, a protagonist with a self-consciously performed identity and feelings of emptiness behind the performance. While Highsmith's psychopath suggests a violence and sadism at the core of the empty consumerism that characterizes postwar life, *Dexter*, in contrast, participates in a circus of cruelty offering anti-social identifications as a promise of negotiating a failed sociality. While Highsmith's work illustrates the impossibility of a social world organized around psychopathic traits and the violence of consumer capitalism and the class system, *Dexter* shares with action films a worldview in which the violence of the social can only be adequately met with the private exceptional violence of the psychopath outside of the failed public sphere.

Ripley

Patricia Highsmith's series of Ripley novels spanned the cold war with *The Talented Mr. Ripley* published in 1955 and the last of five books, *The Boy who Followed Ripley,* appearing in 1990. Two novels, *The Talented Mr. Ripley* and *Ripley's Game,* were made into films. The Ripley novels followed Highsmith's success from her book *Strangers on a Train* which Hitchcock made into a popular film. Thematically, *Strangers on a Train* shares with the Ripley novels a focus on characters who learn to kill without conscience. In *Strangers on a Train,* however, the characters free themselves from conscience by switching murders—they meet on a train, share their grievances, and agree each to perform the killing of the other's adversary. In the Ripley novels, on the other hand, Highsmith puts both the feeling of transgression and the pursuit of reprieve in the character's development, with the narration working through the problem of what a character looks like who kills without remorse. Ultimately, though, the killer in *Strangers on a Train* gives himself away to the police authorities by displaying his guilt. Highsmith's future narratives struggle to resolve this problem of how to get away with murder and perform the "perfect crime" without revealing the secret. The answer to this "problem" of conscience lies in performing impersonation so thoroughly that one becomes the person being impersonated. One can avoid suspicion and detection by projecting a confidence earned through total identification with an other who one has become. Guilt, conscience, and responsibility can be sloughed off or externalized along with the prior personality.

Highsmith illustrates how one dissolves conscience, exculpating responsibility and guilt through identification with a fictional other. Guilt and responsibility for destructively self-interested behavior can be sloughed off or "externalized" like the identity position left behind. The novels cover Thomas Ripley's development from provincial American, middle class, sexually confused, insecure young man to the role of confident, bourgeois, cosmopolitan, killer and art forger. One of Ripley's talents is impersonation. In the first novel, he falls in love with and then kills and impersonates Dickie Greenleaf. Dickie's father has hired Ripley to find Dickie in Italy and convince him to return home to his family, boat building business, and conventional 1950s lifestyle. Instead of convincing Dickie to return, Tom reveals the father's plot and emulates Dickie's lugubrious expat ruling class lifestyle of leisure: sunbathing, painting, boating, partying, and traveling in Europe. Tom first inserts himself into Dickie's relationship with his girlfriend, Marge. When Dickie tires of Tom's company, refusing to drop Marge and spurning his affection, Tom kills Dickie on a motorboat, takes his fine things, and he impersonates Dickie for many months. During this time, he kills Dickie's friend Freddie Miles to avoid discovery. Tom forges a will to capture Dickie's inheritance and reluctantly abandons his assumed identity of Dickie. In the later novels, Tom has added to his income and supported his penchant for the good life by marrying a French heiress of an industrial chemical fortune. Additional income derives from his conspiracy to forge new paintings by a dead artist named Derwatt and to create several businesses from the artist's renown. Tom also dabbles in smuggling and exchanges favors with a shadowy connection in Germany named Reeves Minot. In *Ripley Under Ground,* after impersonating Derwatt (who is dead but said to be in Mexico), Tom kills an American businessman named Murchison who is on to the Derwatt forgeries. In *Ripley Under Water* and in *Ripley's Game,* Tom's killing follows from complicated schemes in response to his being insulted. In the last novel, *The Boy who Followed Ripley,* Tom kills to protect a boy killer who admires and emulates him.

Scholarship on Ripley has focused on the performance of identity in the Highsmith novels without historicizing the idea of identity with the problem of conscience that the novels raise.[16] Like a method actor, Ripley becomes those he impersonates believing that the small details of affect, manner, and clothing "make the person." The literature has largely side-stepped, however, the object relations dimensions of Ripley. Ripley loves things and can only love other people as things. He must kill—that is, inanimate the loved other such as Dickie Greenleaf—and then incorporate Dickie into himself through impersonation. Tom loves himself as Dickie, luxuriating in his things and carefree cultural capital, but despises himself as anxious, middle class, poorly dressed Tom Ripley. Ripley is radically alienated, realizing prior to murdering Dickie that he will always be alone and cannot ever truly connect with or love or be loved by others. Through the murder and impersonation of Dickie, Tom achieves class ascension. That is, Ripley's class elevation is effected through crime rather than through aristocratic inheritance (like Dickie, Marge, and Heloise) or meritocratic upward mobility—inclusion into a corporate dominated economy through submission to the rules of the game. Ripley makes his own rules for how to live. He represents desire freed of middle class mores, self-limitation, and morality that would check his ambition for having things and free time.[17] Ripley embodies Mill's *Homo oeconomicus* defined by advancing one's interest through icy calculation. Like the person of the corporation, Ripley has no checks on his desire, no moral code, no deep commitments to anyone beyond himself (all commitments are strategic), no conscience, and no guilt. He is an elevated consumerist survival machine capable of morphing into different forms to achieve the scheme of the moment.

Highsmith asks her reader to identify with the profoundly amoral character of the psychopath's consciousness. She pushes an obvious disjuncture between the reader's sense of right and desire for Ripley's success. Ripley is a tantalizing monster who is enviable to the reader for being cultured, for being free and smart, and for his nice things—his Gucci luggage, his Alfa Romeo, and his chateaus. His lack of convictions or deep passions makes him profoundly unheroic and, coupled with his affected ruling class lugubriousness, even boring. In a sense, Highsmith is an anti-Ayn Rand, illustrating a world in which the radically self-interested and conscienceless behavior performed by Ripley is thoroughly anti-social and could never be universalized. As well, the world of bourgeois privilege is one largely acquired by lucky inheritance and, in Tom's case, by crime.

Highsmith shows us a world in which meritocratic ideology is rendered suspect at best. In the context of inherited privilege of his ruling class peers, Tom's class mobility through forgery appears more as a strategy for gaming the class structure than it does an injustice.

In *Civilization and its Discontents* Freud describes the "oceanic feeling" of connectedness of the self to the universe. In Freud the infant's initial unalienated state is an experience of the undifferentiated ego with no separation from the mother's body and the rest of the world. The denial of the breast initiates the break, individuation, alienation. It is no coincidence that water plays a recurring role in the Ripley novels as that which swallows up Tom's lost love objects. Tom's parents drowned in Boston Harbor in an accident, leaving him to be raised by an unloving and cruel aunt. He kills Dickie on a motorboat and buries him in the sea. Tom's psychopathology is the result of the loss of the loved objects of his parents. Tom seeks to overcome his extreme aloneness by uniting with Dickie. Dickie's rejection brings Tom to the realization that he will never overcome aloneness. This realization precipitates the murder, as the only solution to Tom's isolation is for Tom and Dickie to be one person. By killing Dickie, Tom also kills himself. In *Escape from Freedom,* Erich Fromm, building on Freud, describes the sadomasochistic relation. Fromm explains that individuals experience repeated trials of separation from others throughout life. The growth of individual strength separates one from others and how one forges new social relations to overcome alienation can be productive (through creative work or love) or destructive (through sadism and masochism). For the sadist, love can only be achieved by having the other, controlling the other, consuming and incorporating the other—overcoming alienation by annihilating the other. Killing the other is the ultimate act of controlling the other by making the other inanimate. It is the dynamic changing nature of others that defies control.

Tom exemplifies the masochistic abandonment of self described by Fromm (the desire to be absorbed into and obliterated by the other—to overcome the distance of alienation by abdicating the self) as well as the sadistic aim for total control of the other. As well, Tom typifies what Fromm describes as the replacement of being with having in consumer capitalism. Unable to feel love for others, Tom passionately loves jewelry, furniture, clothing, and homes. Ripley's consumerism is not the middle class one of the endless acquisition and disposal of consumer goods but rather the acquisition of select things.

> Evenings looking at his clothes—his clothes and Dickie's—and feel-
> ing Dickie's rings between his palms, and running his fingers over

the antelope suitcase he had bought at Gucci's. He had polished the suitcase with a special English leather dressing, not that it needed polishing because he took such good care of it, but for its protection. He loved possessions, not masses of them, but a select few that he did not part with. They gave a man self-respect. Not ostentation but quality, and the love that cherished the quality. Possessions reminded him that he existed, and made him enjoy his existence. It was as simple as that. And wasn't that worth something? He existed.

(TMR, 249)

In the 1980s, Brett Easton Ellis' *American Psycho* continues this theme, situating the equation of consumerism with violent psychopathology in the Reagan era and its obsession with brands. Ellis' character is a narcissistic monster without a fleshed out motivation. In the 1990s, Chuck Palahniuk's *Fight Club* illustrates in an unfortunately sexist way the deadening, maddening, and emasculating experience of life reduced to having. The result in this case is a schizophrenic split in which an out of control alter ego pursues anti-capitalist mayhem through a quasi-fascist political movement before being discovered and killed off by the protagonist. In *Ripley*, Highsmith illustrates a fundamental horror of consumer capitalism by collapsing having and being. Being is only having. It is as simple as that.

Is not the horror of the powerful, predatory, self-aggrandizing person emptied of care for other people, emptied of responsibility to others, emptied of conscience, the horror of corporate personhood? Part of the way corporations signify personhood is in how they are able to separate from the actual person, taking the form of a person in the very act of squeezing out the content. Ripley solves the problem of conscience by becoming the other emptied of content but full of costly signifiers such as the rings, the clothes, the gait, the pronunciation. Essence is in the possession of incidentals and in the possession of gestures. As Tom realizes, "Hadn't he learned something from these last months? If you wanted to be cheerful, or melancholic, or wistful, or thoughtful, or courteous, you simply had to act those things with every gesture" (TMR, 193). Having killed Dickie, Tom earns confidence finally through having Dickie's things and the things he can have with Dickie's money:

Tom had an ecstatic moment when he thought of all the pleasures that lay before him now with Dickie's money, other beds, tables, seas, ships, suitcases, shirts, years of freedom, years of pleasure. Then he turned the light out and put his head down and almost at once fell asleep, happy, content, and utterly confident, as he had never been before in his life.

(TMR, 112)

The promise of freedom, happiness, and confidence through the possession of the right things and gestures is the promise that the corporation makes to the individual in consumer capitalism. Omnipresent advertising, public relations, product placement, and consumer fantasies work to instantiate an ambivalent consumer identity at the core of the self—lack/desire—you lack this one thing which would install you in the symbolic fantasy space but the act of consumption promises fulfillment. Consumer pedagogies succeed in replacing our consciences with a self defined through having things, enacting the right gestures, and impersonating the elevated fantasy figures of consumption. The survival and flourishing of personhood for corporations depends on the way that flesh and blood people identify with the brand of the corporation and its associated fantasy world. Moreover, people learn to assent to corporate power, environmental despoliation, and human exploitation by sharing with the corporation the logic of impersonation and externalization in which *to be* is always a promise of *being someone else* who is defined by having and by always having more.

If the Ripley novels reflect the limits of *Homo oeconomicus* by exposing the pathologies in the world he assumes, then the television series *Dexter* provides a very different point of identification with predation.

Dexter

A Showtime original series, *Dexter* was broadcast from 2006 to 2013 and was inspired by Jeff Lindsay's novel *Dreaming Dexter Darkly*. The serial killing protagonist Dexter witnessed the violent murder of his mother at the age of three and developed the characteristics of a violent psychopath as a child. His adoptive father Harry noticed Dexter's tendencies and taught him a code for living with and concealing his impulses from others. Throughout the series Dexter lives by "Harry's Code" which allows him to largely limit his serial killing to those who "deserve it." Dexter is a vigilante serial killer who mostly only kills other killers.

Dexter shares with the Ripley novels a focus on a radically isolated protagonist who desperately wants to connect to others but knows that such connection is impossible. Dexter understands his disconnection from others as a function of hiding his secret unquenchable biological urge to kill, an urge which he refers to as his "dark passenger." Like Ripley, Dexter's identity is a performance. Yet, while Ripley's performance does not have an authentic self behind it (Tom Ripley is a performance), Dexter's killer self is the stable identity that needs to be concealed. *Dexter* largely relies on the biological determinist explanation for Dexter's behavior, suggesting that his predisposition as a psychopath was shaped in a particular direction by his experience of his mother's murder. Dexter's brother, also a serial killer, is represented as also having the biological predisposition, yet, having experienced the mother's murder at a later age, has no capacity to modulate and limit his serial killing impulse the way Dexter does. Dexter's authentic killer persona is intimately shared with the viewer through narrative voiceovers that mostly occur when Dexter is alone driving or disposing of a body on his boat or pursuing a victim. He depressively ruminates over the curse of his dark passenger and over his inability to really connect with others because of his need to keep his killings secret.

Dexter works for the Miami Dade police as a civilian employee specializing in blood spatter patterns for the homicide division. His job allows him access to research of his own future victims, and his own victims frequently intersect with the high profile cases being worked by homicide. The show suggests that the law of the state is largely ineffectual relative to the private code of the killer. Moreover, the means of upholding the law of the state are constituted when private individuals connected to the state break the law in the interests of security. This logic accords with the trend of the federal government since 9/11 to break both domestic and international law in the name of national security. It also accords with the neoliberal tendency to portray the government as failed in order to justify privatization, contracting, outsourcing, and deregulation.

As a figure with which to identify, Dexter shares with countless action hero vigilantes a promise of transgression in the service of conservative morality, of upholding the social order through the enforcement of retribution. Ripley kills to become his loved object, to attain his life of having things, or to conceal his impersonations and forgeries. Dexter has to kill and so he channels his murderous uncontainable impulse that stems from his broken biology merged with his experience of violent loss of his mother. In *Dexter*, only by breaking the law can the moral law be upheld. The seductiveness of such a promise for the viewer is that it invests exceptional godlike moral authority in each person. For spectators to identify with Dexter is to assume the fantasy space of god. Justice, in this view, cannot be achieved through community deliberation or collectively enacted legislation. Nor does justice require checks and balances and public oversight. In fact, public oversight is an impediment to justice in Dexter. A profoundly anti-democratic view, justice here is the preserve for the few with strong wills and strong enough bodies. *Dexter* asks viewers to accept justice through the assumptions and values of totalitarianism. Justice as it is expressed in *Dexter* is the justice of the secret police.

Dexter is an attractive character. He dresses stylishly, is handsome, feels care for his family. Most importantly he inverts the most inhuman brutality by bringing the viewer into intimacy with his ongoing existential crisis and loneliness. He confides in and confesses his true feelings in narrative voiceover only to the viewer. If Ripley kills and impersonates the longed for other, Dexter positions the viewer as the longed for other who can merge with Dexter through shared secrets, intimate details, and a blood lust that no one else can know. Like Ripley, Dexter desires to inanimate his victims. Dexter treats his victims as disposable consumer goods, like meat in a supermarket ready for consumption: he wraps his victims in plastic wrap on a table and stabs them in the heart. He universally dismembers them, disposing of them in garbage bags, and dumps them in the sea. Yet, unlike Ripley, Dexter's murders are not motivated by a desire to impersonate his victims, to abandon himself and unite with them. Rather, Dexter repeatedly kills himself off symbolically in the act of killing other serial killers.

Dexter's killing is sadistic in that it allows for temporary control over the dark passenger. Like consumerism, Dexter's dark passenger is an unquenchable thirst to consume, destroy, dispose. Consuming his victims only briefly assuages his frustrating desire for more. Dexter's victims are bad product, society's spoilage, and he is merely "taking out the trash." The vast majority of Dexter's victims are radically objectified as deviant monsters even before he cuts them into dismembered objects. In a historical moment in which entire populations, the poor, and the homeless are treated as disposable, unworthy of social investment, and blamed for being positioned as such, Dexter encourages a brutal view of the social as populated by unknowable monsters who should be secretly killed.[18]

Dexter as a character exhibits the traits of corporate personhood. *Dexter* not only offers up a predatory character for identification in this predatory economic climate but it also suggests as natural and inevitable privatized solutions to a naturalized violence of the social world. The violence of financial capital, the violence of state enforced property interests, and the symbolic violence of racism do not exist. Instead, violence is largely a biological effect. The denial of social causes of violence paired with a privatized solution to naturalized violence produces an understanding of social violence in which public action and policy decisions play no part. The only relation to violence in this picture for the viewer becomes one of the spectator who is brought into intimacy with Dexter, the agent of privatized "justice." The pedagogy of *Dexter* affirms alienation as inevitable, promising agency only through a fantasy of being the ultimate predator in an inevitably violent society of exclusion.

Conclusion

In this chapter, I have argued that we ought to build on Joel Bakan's insight that corporate personhood is psychopathic by recognizing the pedagogies of the corporation that educate individuals into psychopathic social relations. I have drawn on the novels of Patricia Highsmith because she illustrates the social limits of psychopathic traits. There can be no society of psychopaths. Moreover, Highsmith highlights the way that identity in consumer capitalism operates through impersonation and externalization of conscience, guilt, and responsibility as individuals are defined through having. She paints a disturbing, horrifying, and prophetic picture of amoral sociality. I have discussed *Dexter* as exemplary of a newly celebrated predatory culture and selfhood at a historical moment of predatory politics and economy.

Fromm reminds us that the historical possibility for consciousness and criticality were made possible by the alienation and objectification that capitalist development fostered. In the era organized by pillage and predation, creativity and critical thought are being harnessed in the service of making empty selves defined by having. The problem of corporate personhood is not only the removal of responsibility from those who control capital and the abdication of social responsibility for destructive effects. Regulating corporate behavior and repealing the legality of corporate personhood would be socially valuable steps towards the end of limiting the tendencies of corporations to externalize destruction on the public and educate individuals into the values of competitive acquisition, consumerism, and the traits of psychopathy. Such steps would need to contribute to a broader effort to end the division between corporate work and corporate ownership and replace it with the democratic arrangement of shared labor and decision-making for shared benefit. As well, this chapter has suggested that the inevitable meaning-making practices of cultural workers and educators matter tremendously in producing the identifications and subject positions for youth and all people to occupy. Critical educators and cultural workers can offer youth not only the theoretical tools to analyze and interpret cultural products. They can also do the crucial pedagogical and political work of producing cultural forms and identifications defined by social, caring, just, egalitarian and democratic values and aspirations. The narratives, ideologies, and identifications we make matter for enabling criticism of an unjust present as well as for imagining and building a better future.

Notes

1 Joel Bakan, *The Corporation: The Pathological Pursuit of Profit and Power* New York: Free Press, 2005. Bakan co-wrote the documentary film *The Corporation* directed by Mark Achbar, 2005.

2 M. Levenson, K. Kiehl, C. Fitzpatrick "Assessing Psychopathic Attributes in a NonInstitutionalized Population" *Journal of Personality and Social Psychology* 68(1) (1995), 151–8.

3 These examples are all taken up in detail in both the book and film *The Corporation*.

4 Jared A. DeFife, "Predator on the Prowl" in *The Psychology of Dexter* edited by Bella Depaulo, Dallas: BenBella Books, 2010, 7.

5 See Jean Baudrillard *The Consumer Society* Thousand Oaks, CA: Sage, 1970, and the work of Sut Jhally including his films with the Media Education Foundation.

6 The film *The Corporation* illustrates this point well through the examples of Kathy Gifford's sweatshop apparel manufacturing practices and BP's pollution. Coca-Cola's water privatization, use of paramilitaries against labor unionists, and other abuses have been documented by the Killer Coke campaign. Self-imposed "social responsibility" codes cannot be relied upon when the demand for profits runs contrary to human interests and the media spotlight turns to other spectacles.

7 Robert Hare, *Snakes in Suits* New York: HarperBusiness, 2006.

8 See, for example, Kent A. Kiehl and Joshua Buckholtz "Inside the Mind of a Psychopath" *Scientific American Mind* 21(4) (2010), 22–9.

9 See Thomas Lemke, *Biopolitics: An Advanced Introduction* New York: NYU Press, 2011, 18.

10 Kiehl and Buckholtz "Inside the Mind of a Psychopath," 22–9.

11 Cary Federman, Dave Holmes, and Jean Daniel Jacob, "Deconstructing the Psychopath: A Critical Discursive Analysis" *Cultural Critique* 72 (2009), 36–65.

12 See Nick Couldry, "Reality TV, or the Secret Theater of Neoliberalism" *The Review of Education Pedagogy Cultural Studies* 30(1) (2008), 3–13. For a link to the theater of cruelty and public pedagogy see Henry Giroux, *Youth in a Suspect Society: Democracy or Disposibility?* New York: Palgrave Macmillan, 2010.

13 Robin Truth Goodman and Kenneth Saltman, *Strange Love, Or How We Learn to Stop Worrying and Love the Market* Lanham, MD: Rowman & Littlefield, 2002, which discusses these examples at length as cultural pedagogy.

14 See Robin Truth Goodman, *Policing Narratives and the State of Terror.*

15 Michele Byers, "Neoliberal Dexter?" in Douglas Howard (ed.) *Dexter: Investigating Cutting Edge Television* New York: I.B. Tauris, 2010.

16 See, for example, Michael Trask, "Patricia Highsmith's Method" *American Literary History* 22(3) (2010), 584–614, and John Dale, "Crossing the Road to Avoid Your Friends: Engagement, Alienation, and Patricia Highsmith" *Midwest Quarterly* 51(4) (2010), 405.

17 This insight comes from Robin Truth Goodman personal communication.

18 For excellent recent discussions of the politics of disposability see Henry Giroux, *Youth in a Suspect Society* New York: Palgrave, 2010; and Zygmunt Bauman *Wasted Lives* New York: Polity, 2005.

CONCLUSION

The preceding chapters have shown how the rise in corporeal control in education involves controlling not just bodies but minds as well. I have illustrated how claims to technological progress and innovation in the forms of big data, surveillance, learning analytics, pharmacology, and repressive pedagogy promote practices that foster anti-democratic social relations and identifications, and unthinking obedience. I have contended that what is at stake here is not merely a threat to critical thinking as problem solving skills, creativity, and individual freedom. What is at stake in the scripting of bodies is a threat to the capacity of individuals to learn in ways that help them comprehend themselves and the society in which they live. Beyond understanding, in the tradition of critical pedagogy I contend that learning needs to foster forms of living that are reflective—reflective about what one does, how the self is socially formed, and how to comprehend and act on and shape the social world. In other words, the question of education cannot be comprehended in terms of the technical efficiencies of delivery of knowledge nor of the development of critical thinking as problem solving skills. Rather, the problem of education is whether public schools can create the conditions for a thinking society capable of democratic self-governance, humane and collective forms of control, and the reduction of arbitrary and authoritarian forms of control.

There are powerful and growing political forces fighting against the repressive trends in education that I have discussed here. A number of these movements seize back control of the body as part of educational justice movements. For example, the opt out movement against high stakes standardized testing continues to build with growing numbers of parents and students refusing to take the PARCC and SBAC tests that correspond to the Common Core State Standards, sometimes by even walking out of school. In Chicago in the fall of 2015 parents and community members conducted a 34 day hunger strike at Dyett High School, the last open enrollment neighborhood school in Bronzeville on Chicago's southside. Hunger strikers resisted Chicago mayor Rahm Emanuel's plans to close the neighborhood school and make it into an arts academy while also calling for community control and a school and curriculum plan organized around a progressive vision for ecology and technology.

The Chicago Teachers Union's Caucus of Rank and File Educators have been a model for expanding the struggle for public education against neoliberal restructuring by linking matters of labor not just to broader educational issues like school funding and resistance to privatization but also by linking them to broader economic, cultural, and political matters such as neoliberalism, poverty, unemployment, environmental sustainability, and racism. In New York City the Movement of Rank and File Educators similarly push for such linkages as do the Massachusetts Association of Teachers under Barbara Madeloni discussed in Chapter 4 who has taken aim at corporatization, testing, and edTPA. Similarly, in Chile, Quebec, and elsewhere students are linking resistance to neoliberal education with resistance to the neoliberal model and austerity politics generally.

It is crucial for teachers and their unions, students, and citizens to follow the lead of these principled and progressive educators who see the links not just between educational issues and broader social struggles but also value educational theory as a crucial tool for teachers and leaders to examine the values, assumptions, and ideologies animating policies and practices.

As I have argued throughout this and prior books, the depoliticized liberal defense of public education is inadequate for addressing the corporatization of schools in part because it fails to adequately comprehend the relationships between formal schooling, learning, and the broader social realities, structures, and struggles that inform and give meaning to the lives of students and teachers. Liberals have recently begun repackaging a depoliticized approach to pedagogy that emphasizes process and critical thinking. Linda Darling-Hammond, among others, for example, has been promoting "deeper learning," which refers to the transmission of "content knowledge," critical thinking and analytical skills, and the transfer of analytical skills to different subjects. While "deeper learning" appears preferable to the banking education models inherent in high stakes standardized testing, it nonetheless promotes a form of learning in which knowledge is not taken up in relation to broader questions of power, politics, ethics, and history or in relation to the subjective experience of the student that is formed by these objective social forces. Deeper learning is not deep enough. Learning needs to be related to the material and symbolic interests and struggles behind claims to truth in the traditions of critical education. For this reason cultural conservative approaches to school reform that emphasize the transmission of dogma and fundamentalisms should also be rejected. Various cultural conservative efforts promote Eurocentric historical and literary canons, and religious anti-science rejections of evolution and sex education. Local control is not enough. The partial shift to local control presented by the federal partial retreat on high stakes standardized testing coming with the Every Student Succeeds Act provides an opening to reactionary approaches to education. Critical educators have to seize this opening and organize movements to fight against reactionary and anti-democratic fundamentalisms and against positivist and de-politicized liberal reforms. Critical educators can work instead to develop and institutionalize critical educational approaches to curriculum and pedagogy that aim to remake broader social institutions in deeply egalitarian ways.

While this book details the rise of repression in school, it would be a mistake to turn to other emancipatory promises that are depoliticized like deeper learning or depoliticized versions of teacher preparation framed through "professionalization." For example, against the rigidity and structuring of time and knowledge, the vocationalism, the gutting of recess, and behaviorist hand gestures of KIPP's SLANT program, it is not enough to call for recess, free time, or return to the free school movement with its total abdication of pedagogical authority over the curriculum. Students bring in to school values and knowledge that need to be questioned for their underlying assumptions and animating ideologies. Teachers and administrators are always in a position to affirm or contest the ideologies that youth express. There is no way out of the inevitably political role of teaching and administrating. Consequently, to deny the political positions that one takes is itself a political move that affirms existing arrangements, values, and ideologies. While the rise of repression in education represents a hostility to play, it would be a mistake to conceive of freedom from repressive control as simply the removal of control. Teachers and administrators need to comprehend better, more egalitarian forms of non-repressive control that enable collective forms of agency. There is great value in the development of learned self-discipline for youth to cultivate the dispositions for sustained investigation of problems, for thoughtful engagement with texts, and for multiple forms of interpretation and judgment. However, these dispositions cannot be comprehended as tools for knowledge accumulation and exchange, and ultimately assimilation into existing institutions of power. To be meaningful they need to be understood as part of a project for understanding, problematizing, and remaking the self and society. The partial retreat on high stakes standardized testing in the form of the Every Student Succeeds Act of 2015 is a small step in the right direction. However, the modest latitude over assessment afforded states and locales ought to be seen as an opportunity to pursue a critical and intellectual form of teaching and learning that fosters habits of curiosity, dialogue, and dissent that are not only the basis for critical and creative thought but that are also essential for a democratic society. Educational policies guiding teacher certification and preparation, state and national standards need to be changed to link knowledge to both subjectivity (lived experience) and objectivity (the broader social world) in ways that take seriously the constitutive class and cultural antagonisms that structure the self and the social. Rather than taking up knowledge, teaching and learning in relation to power and politics, unfortunately the details of the Every Student Succeeds Act use federal funding to promote the privatization of teacher and leader preparation in forms that remain linked to positivist standardized testing and that move towards vocationalism and the "methods fetish," and away from the pedagogical, curricular, and social theory found in the best critical university-based preparation programs. The act also funds alternative assessments that measure grit and other "social emotional" dispositions. Resisting these tendencies and expanding critical pedagogies will require creativity and intellectual work on the part of teachers, administrators, and citizens.

Teachers unions, social movements, and activists need to embrace the reality that the battle against the unwarranted control of the body must fully reckon with the struggle for the mind. To treat education as a preparation for potential inclusion into existing radically unequal and exclusionary institutions such as the economy and the electoral system offers no way for education to be a force for social reinvention. Public schools, despite the steady tightening of repressive controls and sense of insecurity, must be seen still as a site and stake of struggle for a genuinely democratic society. Such a project requires schools to be able to provide the intellectual tools for social and ideological analysis, for critical consciousness, and to question and transform culture and common sense. As Stanley Aronowitz and Henry Giroux have contended, schools must be places that can foster the radical imagination. Schooling cannot be reduced to teaching knowledge and skills. Critical pedagogy and other forms of critical education are essential tools for schools to foster ways of denouncing a present structured in oppression and exploitation and to create the conditions to imagine a radically different and freer future.

INDEX